MW01088088

$OLO CONTENDERE

How to Go Directly from Law School
Into the Practice of Law
Without Getting a Job

Third Edition

by
Marc D. Garfinkle, Esq.

©2010 Marc D. Garfinkle, Esq.
All Rights Reserved
2070 Millburn Avenue
Maplewood, NJ 07040
973-275-1313

ISBN 978-0-9843801-2-1

"Lavi long fe we."

Haitian proverb:
"A long life lets you see."

Books and ebooks available at
www.SoloContendere.com and selected bar associations.

Special pricing consideration available for bar associations,
CLE programs, law school bookstores and U.S. veterans.

For seminars and CLE workshops helping new lawyers to go solo,
or for lawyer skills enhancement programs, visit Marc Garfinkle's
www.BetterTestimony.com.

For

Eylana, Yaël and Jordan

$OLO CONTENDERE *3ʳᵈ Ed.*

How to Go Directly from Law School
Into the Practice of Law – *Without* Getting a Job

by Marc D. Garfinkle, Esq.

Foreword

Breaking the Ice

Foreword to the Second Edition

In law schools from coast to coast, students are panicking. Law firms and agencies that traditionally hired thousands of recent grads each year are not hiring. Others are deferring the hiring of graduates to whom jobs had already been offered. Law firms are trimming their staffs to survive the economic downturn which has caused an unprecedented reduction in the demand for lawyers.

These developments are frightening for young lawyers in the job market who have invested heavily or borrowed mightily in order to pay for law school. A few years ago, there was little reason for them to imagine a dearth of job opportunities at this end. Now, many don't know where to turn. They are disillusioned and disoriented. Some look for jobs in tangential fields; others in unrelated fields. Some wonder whether they will ever get to practice law at all.

This book is for lawyers who want to work for themselves, even if they have never worked as lawyers before, and even if they just passed the Bar last week.

It is based on two premises:

1. You do not need to have a *job* in order to practice law; all you really need is *work*.

2. With appropriate precautions, you can be an effective, even excellent attorney, despite your lack of experience, or maybe because of it.

There is nothing so complicated about practicing law that you can't learn it on the job. That's how we *all* learned our trade. That's how you will, too. You don't need to know all the answers, but you must know what the questions are. Appreciate how much you *don't* know. You know what you know, but you don't know what you don't know. Therein lies your greatest danger as a solo.

Fortunately, resources abound. Court rules and case law will point you in the right direction. County clerks, court officers, "records room" people and judges' secretaries will be helpful, too, once you figure out what you want and how to ask for it nicely. Ditto that for other attorneys, even your adversaries. Superb resources are there for you. We will point you toward a few of the best. They will lead you to many more. Use them.

You *can* make a living as a lawyer without getting a job, as long as you know your stuff, keep good counsel, and watch your depth. You'll gain experience quickly. Hang on! Done correctly, you should be able to enjoy the journey as well as the destination.

Dangers, both obvious and hidden, await you as a new attorney going solo into the jungle. Take heart that there are simple ways to protect yourself and your clients as you venture forth. Maintain adequate malpractice insurance. Develop access to experienced lawyers and go to them frequently for counsel. Treat everyone with civility. Read and understand the ethics rules and apply them to your business and personal lives.

Be prepared to undertake the caseload of a lawyer and the responsibilities of a business owner. Look out for conflicts of interest and avoid even the appearance of impropriety. Be prudent in the cases you accept. Be obsessive about returning your phone calls and emails. Review all of your files frequently, and stay in touch with your clients. Confirm darn near everything in writing.

Despite its many warnings and its decidedly defensive approach, this book is not a guide to avoiding failure. It is a handbook on how to succeed, a blueprint for building a practice. Unfortunately, it is no substitute for having great business contacts, a bottomless trust fund, your "retirement case," or uncanny luck, but it may give you some tools and insights and confidence. Good luck. And please let me know how it goes.

Marc D. Garfinkle

$olo Contendere

How to Go Directly from Law School
Into the Practice of Law - *Without* Getting a Job

by Marc D. Garfinkle, Esq.

I.

You Can Afford to Go Solo

Lawyers Don't Need Jobs

We need work. We need clients who will pay us to do the things that lawyers do. It's really that simple. Whatever your circumstance, whatever your means, there is a way for you to start practicing law in the immediate future, if you really want to.

It doesn't matter that law firms are not hiring. You shouldn't care that there are more lawyers than ever. You don't need a job. If you can get in your thirty or so hours of lawyering each week, you can do very well. How you go about doing it depends on your individual circumstance.

It doesn't matter whether you are rich or poor (although rich helps). Maybe you have money in the bank; maybe you don't. Perhaps you already have a great full-time job. Maybe you have a part-time job you hate. Maybe you've never had a job. Perhaps there is a family business you can rely on to save you, or perhaps you are staring at a crushing debt from education loans. Some young lawyers can live rent-free with their parents, but maybe you have two mortgages and child support to pay. Maybe your spouse earns a zillion dollars or you have a generous pension from your last job. Rich or poor, you can do it. Don't heed the cynics.

Look to start a practice in a way that accommodates your economic and familial circumstance. Consider the various office arrangements and types of practices to see what best suits your situation. Investigate them. Then decide on your course of action. These factors will dictate many of your costs.

You may not need a lot of money to get started on your own, but you will certainly need *some*. Your usual living expenses will not go on vacation while your practice gets started, and the start-up itself could be costly. Once you determine the sort of practice you wish and the sort of office you'll look for, you can calculate what your usual monthly payments will be. Will there be rent? Employees? Postage? Case costs? Taxes and fees? Memberships? Insurance? Accountant? Assistant? Part-timers? Internet? Website? CLE? Relax. You can do it.

Once you have an understanding of your regular expenses, figure out what your start-up costs might be, allowing a thick cushion for the unknown. Talk to other lawyers about their growing pains. Although you may have smooth sailing from the first, you will probably have to endure some slow times, especially in the beginning. Keep a close eye on expenses.

To Whom Can You Turn?

To become both a successful lawyer and business-owner all at once, there is much you need to know. You are not expected to know everything, but you must know where to find it out. You must have handy access to legal resources and office resources. You will need access to legal data bases and other research tools. You are expected to have a computer and to know how to use it. There are classes to take. There is so much to learn before you can be comfortable in either role.

Above all, you must have colleagues who can serve as mentors or sounding boards for your ideas. They are not optional. They will protect you against errors and malpractice, and they will give you the benefit of their experience. You will need at least one such lawyer even on your very first case. We discuss how to find and cultivate these people, below.

Happily for you, many state, county and local bar associations have committees devoted to the interests and needs of small and solo practices. Check them out. They usually have willing and able volunteer mentors available, in addition to providing helpful literature and educational programs. Take advantage of these services. Often, these committees provide excellent networking opportunities for attorneys and serve as showcases for vendors who market products and services to small law firms and solos.

Contact your law school placement, career or alumni offices to learn whether they have a mentoring network in place for alums. Don't be shy about calling each name offered. If you are politely turned down, ask the attorney if s/he has a friend or colleague who might not mind your calling from time to time for free information and advice.

There are many books and blogs and websites that provide resources and specific information to solos. Carolyn Elefant's book *"Solo by Choice"* has helped and encouraged many attorneys to take the less-travelled road. Her website, MyShingle.com, is chockablock with free information and inspiration for lawyers going, or contemplating going, solo.

Soloing guru Jay Foonberg's has helped over a generation of new solos to get started. Check out Foonberglaw.com.

If you enjoy a webinar format, Susan Cartier Liebel's <u>SoloPracticeUniversity</u> may be for you. The "university" comprises interesting and authoritative courses for solos in digital formats. Pithy, well-chosen, and easy-to-read blogs make this site worth bookmarking. Both Elefant and Foonberg are on the "faculty".

The ABA's webpage, "SoloSez" is also a rich source of free information for solos and small firms. Bookmark it. Use it.

Should You Give Up Your Day Job?

There is no reliable formula to figure out how much capital you will need in order to go solo. A guideline might be that you should be able to cover all costs and meet your expenses for nine months, *assuming zero income* during that period. If you can, you may have enough support to proceed confidently without a supplemental source of income. Of course, you can expect to make at least *some* money in the first three quarters, maybe even a lot, but figure conservatively.

"(M)any state, county and local bar associations have committees devoted to... small and solo practices. Check them out"

If you need a steady income from the start, perhaps you can manage with a part-time job. A part-time job to supplement your legal career need not be law-related employment. It doesn't have shine on your C.V. What matters is whether you can integrate that job into your life as a lawyer. What also matters is whether you can get "benefits." There will always be a trade-off: Can you juggle a job and your law career, or is your time better spent pounding the pavement and building the practice?

Having a regular part-time job in the beginning may be just the bridge you need to get to your career. But remember that the time you spend working for someone else, especially in a non-legal situation, usually does not advance your legal career. There will always be tension between the two. For example, if your "other" job requires that you work bankers' hours, but you want to have a trial practice, you should rethink your strategy.

Time is on Your Side

With the shrinking of the world and the advent of email and text messaging, there are suddenly dozens more working hours available each week than ever before. Get ready to take advantage of most of them. And if an odd schedule suits you, and you don't care to go to court, you can even fashion a nocturnal law practice, built around your computer and a coffee pot.

After all, drafting contracts and wills, reviewing files, preparing briefs, drafting correspondence, sending emails and so much more – can be done at night. It often is. If you are able to work through the day and still have the energy to be a lawyer at night, the stars will shine brightly for you.

With some persistence, you may be able to piece together a patchwork of part-time gigs allowing you to earn some regular pay while having the freedom to grow your practice. Don't just look at the lawyer ads. Investigate law-related part-time jobs in service industries and in business. Your legal education gives you a "leg up" at hiring almost anywhere but at law firms. Look for jobs at insurance companies in claims, investigations or risk assessment.

There may be part-time or temporary work for lawyers in copywriting and editing, investigation and security, places that serve alcohol and in casinos. Law grads get hired as full- and part-time title searchers, legal editors, compliance officers, real estate agents and bank tellers. We are highly employable, despite what you hear. Your education has great value in every domain.

Get in the Pool

An outstanding opportunity for part time work exists with many local and county or state Public Defender's office as a "pool attorney" or "conflict lawyer." All criminal courts - federal, state, county and local, are required to offer free or low-cost defense counsel to indigent defendants whose charges expose them to "consequences of magnitude." (NJ) Whether the Public Defender is one person or an office full of attorneys, that office, just like any private office, may not represent more than one defendant in a case. Sometimes several defendants in a case qualify for the PD. That office may not be allowed to represent defendants with conflicts.

The courts usually have budgets for pool attorneys to handle the conflicts. Payment is usually hourly or *per diem*. The work can be fun, and you may find a wealth of mentors among the pool lawyers.

Contact the court administrators or public defenders' offices in your area to learn what pool work may be available and what you must do to apply. Sometimes, the process of getting into the "pool" is highly politicized; usually, it is quite democratic. Pool work has kept both new and experienced lawyers afloat for years.

Also inquire about some specialized pools, which usually require training that is offered by the court or the public defender's office. Many of these programs originate in family or domestic relations court. This pool work may involve representing people who may lose their parental rights, assisting battered women, defending the interests of minors or incompetents, and otherwise serving in a court-appointed capacity. Gaining expertise in a specialized legal niche, especially where a government pays your bill, may be a very good career move.

Do not be put off by the low government pay scale. Talk to other attorneys in the pool. Find out why they do it, how much work they get, whether it helps their private practice.   Some lawyers may be tight-lipped and protective of their domain. Most will be helpful. Find the most helpful ones, and make them your mentors. But check them out. Be careful of your associations.

Learn to Teach

You have a doctoral degree in Law. You must be an expert on *something*.   And while you may not have finished at the top of your class, you still know a whole lot more about the Constitution or Business Law than the average high school or college student. Try teaching, if you think you can. Teaching jobs can be the most rewarding part-time employment you will ever have.   On top of that, the credential is impressive, and the contacts you make may be even more so.

Tailor a separate résumé for teaching jobs. Don't give up. New opportunities appear all the time. Check private schools and colleges for ads seeking lawyers to teach one or two subjects, such as business law or Constitutional law.   Sometimes positions as tutors or substitute teachers are available. Generally, a teaching certificate is not required, and you may make some great local connections. These jobs usually do not pay well, but they are still coveted.

For teaching positions at junior colleges, colleges and universities, the acknowledged best resource is *The Chronicle of Higher Education*, whose postings are available in print and on line at *www.chronicle.com*.

There are, of course, part-time jobs washing dishes, selling auto parts, baking donuts and pumping gas. Other home businesses, often involving pyramid sales or internet marketing, attract entrepreneurial types. All honest work is noble. If you are able to phase out your job as your career "phases in" so much the better. There will be conflicts and growing pains, but keep your eye on the brass ring. Grow your practice.

They don't teach you THIS in law school!

...

Sometimes, you just have to get off the phone.
Maybe nature calls. Your cab is waiting.
When you have NO CHOICE but to hang up on the other person, whomever it is...start saying something with conviction and sincerity, and then, in mid-word, **cut yourself off abruptly.**
It works. Once.

II.

How Are You Going To Do This?

What Do You *Want* to Do (when you grow up)**?**

You are going to work for yourself as a lawyer. Okay – you can do it. Now what? Your earliest planning should address the type of practice you would like and the type of office you will require. Try to envision where you want to be in a year, in five years. Imagine your surroundings, your caseload, your income, your work week. Realistically, can you get there from here?

To answer that, you must consider your tangible options and conservatively estimate your financial strength. Then ask yourself some basic questions: Will you be representing the public or handling work for other lawyers? Will people be coming to you? Will you be going to court? What kind of cases will you handle? Will you specialize? Will you be hiring associates or paralegals? Does the caseload or clientele you seek affect your choice of office location? Do you want to be in walking distance to a lunch spot or to courts? Do you need a fancy address?

Should you have an office in a professional building with all the trappings – receptionist, waiting room, conference room, secretary or paralegal, off-street parking - or should you work from home or in someone else's office? Should you share an office with other solos? How about with non-lawyers? Should you look into those offices you can rent on an "as needed" basis? Options abound; consider several. You may find that you will start out with one vision and gravitate toward another.

Should you work alone or should you work around others? Both options present advantages and disadvantages, and no matter what you do, issues will arise that you didn't consider. Remember, however, that there are important advantages to being in an office where there are other lawyers, especially an office that sends you business. In addition to getting more work from that lawyer or firm, you will be exposed to other attorneys who may be interested in your availability to do work for *them*.

There is the notion that, as the only lawyer in a location, you may get your neighbors' legal work. While that will sometimes be true, working with other lawyers is far more likely to generate billable hours or court appearances for you. And, of course, it is essential to have experienced lawyers around with whom you may discuss your cases, and to whom you may refer the "tough" ones – cases requiring greater expertise or resources than you have.

What is There to Do?

As a solo, you will be inclined to take all sorts of "easy" cases in many fields. Of course, you understand that nothing is easy, but some matters are more *pro forma* and more commonplace than others. Most fields of law comprise matters that can be simple to most any good lawyer, as well as matters that can stump even a longtime expert. "Simple" wills, for example, are routine, and can be reduced to a form, while preparing some other wills may takes months for a team of experts.

A real estate practice can involve the sale of a home, the review of a lease, or the eviction of a tenant. It can also include transactions of the highest level of complexity. A criminal practice can embrace charges such as driving with no insurance, or simple assault, or it can involve the defense of O.J. Simpson's next case..

You can see then, that as a solo, you will be called on to handle matters for clients with diverse legal needs. A few little jobs can keep you afloat. Figure out your rate and your fees, as you will need to charge a real fee for your services. You may be flexible with your fees. Charge by the hour, by the appearance, or by the job. Other lawyers will discuss the "going rates" with you, and you can decide what fees might work for you. You will find work, but you have to promote yourself. Some tips appear below.

Throw in some pool work or public defender work, and you are on your way to a full-time practice. Take the "simple" cases whenever you can, but understand that *nothing* is really simple. Know your depth when you take a case, and get out of it or associate with an expert if it starts to get too deep.

Monitor your own competence and your level of interest in each type of case you handle. You will enjoy some kinds of work and detest others. Then earlier you figure out what you like, the sooner you can develop a plan for referring the cases you don't like to lawyers who don't take the cases *you* like to handle.

When in doubt about whether to keep a case you've already been working on, get help or get out. Attorneys rarely regret "dumping" doubtful cases; we often regret keeping them. Reread the last sentence. Then read the ethics rules on getting out of a case. Put it all in writing to your client. More than once.

Like most lawyers, you will develop a penchant for a particular legal specialty, or an affinity to a particular type of case or client. Your clientele may pull you into areas of the law that you never knew anything about, leading to a specialty to which you'd never given any thought. It happens all the time.

> **"When in doubt... get help or get out.**
> **Attorneys rarely regret "dumping" doubtful cases;**
> **we often regret keeping them.** Reread the last sentence"

For example, your law school roommate may be from a local family that owns a few restaurants. His parents ask you to handle the purchase or sale of their first liquor license. Soon, you do another for the same family or for their friends in the business.

While waiting in the hall at the alcoholic beverage commission for approval on one of your applications, you chat with a lawyer who has done fifty transfers.   She gives you some pointers. You get her card. You send a thank you note in which you ask permission to contact her when you have liquor license questions in the future.   When you follow up on that note, she is gracious.   Your application is approved.   You now have expertise and a mentor. You are almost a specialist.

Another example.   Your friend plays in a garage band, *The Soup Greens*. They won a recording agreement at a Battle of the Bands. They show you their first recording agreement offer, which seems remarkably one-sided against them. Offensively so.   You figure that there must be room for improvement. You do a bit of research. You talk to a few lawyers who know. You learn that the band is not going to get a better deal, that they probably won't make any real money, and that they certainly don't need to spend money which they don't have to hire a Hollywood or New York entertainment law firm which they don't need.   Great. Now what?

They STILL need a lawyer. Why not you?   So you do your homework, you get a small retainer, and you prepare the documents. You run it by a more experienced lawyer who makes some suggestions which you heed. Your client signs the deal, and the band is a moderate success. They get a second deal. This time they're ripe for a "major," a recording company that people have actually heard of. This will involve real money, travel, and agents.

If you do not wish to handle such deals, make an appropriate referral to a colleague or ferret out a list of the best attorneys for your client. Choose a specialist where possible, so that your client will come back to you for all his other needs, knowing that you are honest and fair and are looking out for his interest. Just make sure that your spoon is always in the soup, as not all lawyers will be as ethical as you about soliciting business from other lawyers' clients. But perhaps you don't want to give this case away.

If you'd like to keep your hand in the entertainment field, learn all you can about this sort of work. Then, associate with an experienced entertainment attorney who will "ride shotgun" for you or allow you to "second chair" for her. You should not have to give up too much to do this. Maintain your good relationship with the lead guitarist for *The Soup Greens*, and other lawyers will be glad to be your friend. If you associate with another lawyer, make sure that the work-splitting or fee-sharing agreement you have comports with the ethical rules that pertain, and that your client knows the details of your representation. Put it in writing.

Become an Expert

A legal expert is simply someone with greater knowledge of a particular subject than most other lawyers have. A specialist is an expert who has turned her expertise into a significant part of her practice. If you wish to specialize, you should start by becoming an expert. It takes a while to become a specialist in a field of law. It should take *less* time to become an expert.

One man who is an expert on how to become an expert in *any* field is writer, consultant, speaker and educator Robert W. ("Bob") Bly, who fortunately gives his best advice out for free. Visit his amazing website at www.Bly.com. Bly is also an expert on marketing, social media and writing/publishing.

> **"It takes a while to become a specialist in a field of law. It should take *less* time to become an expert."**

If you enjoy writing, submit articles for internet publication or for professional journals and magazines. There is no better way to get known as an expert. The website, www.Ezine.com, is a perfect vehicle for both new and accomplished authors to build a portfolio.

Teaching a course at a local community college or adult school may be another way for you to demonstrate your expertise, polish your presentation skills, and gain a reputation as an expert. Check out the sorts of classes that are offered, and think of one that you'd like to teach which draws on your expertise.

Send a CV to your local newspapers, cable TV and radio outlets. Let them know that you have some specialized legal knowledge in a particular field, and they might wish to keep your information on file for when they have a case that touches on your expertise. A one-minute DVD may help by showing how photogenic you are or by demonstrating your mellifluent voice. You need not be the world's leading authority to be helpful and interesting to the audience. Once you've been touted as an expert by the media, your credential has been established.

If you want to publish or use print media in any form to grow your practice, or if you want the latest word on legal tech, check out Ari Kaplan's informative and interesting website www.arikaplanadvisors.com. Like Bob Bly, Kaplan offers tons of spot-on information and advice for free. He is also available as a consultant. Any lawyer who seeks to publish should learn what Ari Kaplan has to say.

Should You Specialize?

Okay. You gained some experience with recording contracts or liquor license transfers, and you won't be afraid of the next one at all. In fact, you are beginning to feel like an old pro. You hope that your next case will be the same kind as that. You soon see that most other lawyers do not handle liquor license transfers or recording contracts or whatever else it is that you just did two of. In fact, they may fear, hate or disdain that sort of work. They may be intimidated by it. But you're not.

Now, in conversing with other lawyers, *you* seem to be emerging as a lawyer with specialized knowledge. Others are asking *your* opinion. Is it possible? After only two cases? Is that a specialty? Your future? Is your practice starting to "emphasize" entertainment or liquor license or muni court cases? At what point do you become a specialist? How many hairs make a beard?

Perhaps it's time to review the ethical guidelines that pertain to specialization. You may wish to join a bar association specialty group and receive their journals. Learn whether there Is specialty board certification with requirements you might start looking to fulfill. There are many roads to specialization. None avoids experience.

> **"At what point do you become a specialist?**
> **How many hairs make a beard?"**

Promoting yourself as a specialist is a two-edged sword. Maybe you still enjoy the "general" part of your practice. When you hold yourself out as a specialist, you risk losing business from people who believe you are not interested in cases outside your field. They may not even mention them to you. On the other hand, if you tell the world that you handle a variety of matters, you may not get the call when they think they need a liquor license specialist or a Hollywood lawyer.

One compromise may be to hold yourself out to the public as having a general practice, but *emphasizing* a particular field. For example, in church, you might whisper into the ear of the person in front of you, *"Thanks for asking. I have a general practice, but I'm doing a lot of criminal appeals lately."* or *"I handle all sorts of cases, although I seem to be finding a niche with garage bands and liquor licenses. Maybe I should open a club."* Wait until you're outside before offering your card.

When meeting lawyers, you can bridge the dichotomy by saying, *"I'm a frustrated liquor license lawyer, but until the market comes back, I'm handling most of what comes in the door, and I help other lawyers manage their caseloads. Take my card. Perhaps we can work together."* In the present economy, most lawyers will understand why you are practicing outside your stated area of preference.   They will still remember what you *want* to do, especially if you repeat it when you hand them your card or send a note.   And you should try to send a note to every lawyer who expresses any interest in perhaps working with you in the future.

If you wish to advertise or otherwise publicize a specialty, check your state bar rules to learn the how you may promote it. Some states require certification by a specialty board before a lawyer can be called a "specialist." When you include credentials on your letterhead, your business card, and your marketing material, make sure you comply with court rules and ethical restraints.

Of course, as a specialist, you must continue your legal education and follow the developments in your field(s) of specialization. Having a niche brings its own responsibilities. Keep ahead of the curve in your field. That will make you an expert.

A *Per Diem* Practice

Whether you claim a specialty or not, your most likely sources of work will be other lawyers. Especially in the beginning, you should look for colleagues who need assistance with a heavy caseload, a schedule full of calendar conflicts, files that have become distasteful, or cases that require immediate attention. These lawyers are everywhere, but you must find them and convince them of your worth. They generally won't find *you;* you have to find *them*. You should be able to do this where others have failed.

First, find out what the typical arrangements are in your locale. All sorts of work arrangements are possible, including hourly, *per diem*, per appearance, time-for-space, and others limited only by your creativity. Lawyers loosely call this sort of set-up, "*per diem*" work. It can be a great career. If you are versatile and enjoy variety, you can make yourself available to lawyers as a sort of "go to" person for lawyers. Sell yourself as such. You should get paid as such.

If you have no idea how much to charge, call around or check the local legal newspaper and talk to the per diem lawyers who advertise. You'll soon know the going rate.

Each lawyer has a different expectation of a *per diem* arrangement. Some lawyers may expect you to pick up cases at their office, and expect you to return to *your* office to work on them. Other lawyers will let you use their offices to do your work on their files; some may prefer, or even require that. Some will offer their own resources, such as a conference room, secretarial assistance, photocopying, and other services and facilities that you need while working on *their* clients' cases. Others will expect that you take care of all that yourself and return to them with the finished product. Still others may even let you work on your other cases in their office, if they have the space to spare.

Irrespective of your arrangement, choose your professional affiliations carefully. Check the disciplinary histories of the lawyers with whom you work. You will become known by the company you keep. If most of your work is on behalf of one or two attorneys, other lawyers in your *milieu* will soon associate you with them. Know your bedfellows.

If the *per diem* route works for you, try to develop several, even many, attorney-clients, allowing you some freedom to move around, expanding your network, and further obviating the opening of an office. If you can generate enough hourly or daily billing, you can build your career. You can also develop a specialty this way, with minimal expense and the possibility of substantial income. You might want to give it a try.

Working from Home

If you begin your practice principally as a provider of services to other lawyers, you might be able to shun a traditional office. If you can fill your week doing legal research, appearing in court, attending depositions, briefing or debriefing clients, summarizing files or preparing transactional paperwork, you may not need the amenities of a traditional office.

A "virtual office," a niche in your bedroom with a desk, a phone, a computer with internet access, and a multi-purpose office machine may suffice. You may not need to receive the public, maintain office equipment, store voluminous files or hold conferences at the place where you do your work. Meet the occasional colleague or witness at a library, courthouse or diner. But be warned. While you may be able to do *per diem* work and other work for lawyers from your bedroom niche or virtual office, if you intend to sell your services directly to the public, your office must meet certain minimum criteria.

What passes for an attorney's "office" is not always clear. Some states still require a "brick-and-mortar" office within that state. Others have different standards. Courts and bar associations are currently debating the legality or acceptability of virtual offices. Check your local rules and opinions for recent developments.

Do not assume that your home office is legal merely because the state bar had no objection when you filed your paperwork. Most municipalities require that any such office be zoned for commercial or professional activities. If your office is not authorized by local zoning regulations, it will probably be unacceptable to your state bar. The rules vary widely. Make sure that you understand them before you order your letterhead and business cards.

Also make sure that your home office qualifies for IRS home-business deductions. Of course, you are a lawyer and can probably figure that one out, but call a CPA, anyway. The above notwithstanding, most young solos still aspire to an office of their own. The better you understand the economic and tax consequences of your circumstance, the better you can decide whether you should move from home.

If you work from home, your work space must be secure, and you must have adequate safe storage for your files. Files should be in a keyed room where possible; otherwise, they should be in a locked file cabinet. Doing both is best. Not only must you avoid prying eyes, but you must prevent the loss of paperwork.

> **"You should not use your home computer for your office work if you intend to download, prepare, or transmit client information..."**

The most egregious breaches of client confidences usually occur inadvertently. Keep alert to potential breaches of security. Paper files and computer files should not be accessible to anyone but you and your staff. Even information which appears to be of no use to anyone else may, in fact, be of interest to prying eyes.

You should not use your home computer for your office work if you intend to download, prepare, or transmit client information on that computer, unless you are the sole user. Even then, it's better to have a dedicated computer or network for your practice. Keeping your personal information off your business computer and your business information off your personal computer may prevent you headaches in the future.

If your client's file is being subpoenaed in a fraud case, or if your computer is stolen in a home burglary, you will be glad that you kept your business matters in a separate place. Of course, you should also regularly "back up" your client files, preferably keeping a copy off the premises.

Working with Others

Rarely in your career will you have as much flexibility to change course as you do when you start out. Don't let your office-sharing arrangement be in your way. Before you enter into any sharing arrangement, educate yourself. Check out the space and your space-mates. Learn what you can about the market for office space before you start looking, so you know what a good deal sounds like.

Investigate the ethical histories (usually available online) of the other lawyers in the suite, because you will be known by the company you keep. Find out how long the other lawyers have been sharing the suite, and ask how they get along and whether they exchange referrals. Sometimes, arrangements that start out as office-sharing develop into true partnerships.

You will probably spend a lot of time in your office. Since you may spend at least as much time there as you do at home, it is important that you be comfortable there. Before you sign on with your suite-mates, spend some time around the office. Hang out there, if you can. Feel it out. If you are not satisfied with the way it feels, wait for other options. Trust your gut.

> **"Rarely in your career will you have as much flexibility to change course as you do when you start out. Don't let an office-sharing arrangement be in your way."**

Renting in a legal suite or camping out in another lawyer's office may enable you to reduce overhead while providing you the amenities you need. Various arrangements allow differing levels of autonomy, each of which has pros and cons. It can also facilitate coverage for vacations and scheduling conflicts, and suggest to the public that you are part of a greater whole. Moreover, if your practices differ, you and the other attorneys may prove to be referral sources for each other. Many attorneys have launched successful careers from a desk in someone else's office.

Time for Space

In some office arrangements, you may avoid a rental fee, entirely. You may be able to formulate a "time for space" or similar arrangement with an established office, whereby you agree to work a certain number of hours or to make a certain number of court appearances in exchange for the office space, and, perhaps for services, that you need. Couch your obligation in terms of hours, days or half-days. It can be transposed into dollars for accounting ease. You should state precisely what you will do and what you will get in return. Lawyers respect lawyers who can cut to the chase.

Often you will be given a file with some crazy one-of-a-kind problem you'll remember for years. Sometimes you'll be given a file that two other lawyers had worked on before he took it over. You may have full responsibility for a matter, or you may be on a very short leash.

One thing is sure: you must be "up front" and direct about the money issues that concern you. Find out the details of how you will be paid. How do you get reimbursed for your out-of-pocket expenses such as mileage and photocopy costs that you incur? Does the lawyer expect you to wait until he is paid by his client? Is there a format he prefers for submitting your statement?

Even if it feels awkward to get businesslike in a friendly scenario, just do it. Lawyers are used to it. The awkward moment will pass, and you will avoid misunderstandings later on. This is also the time to talk about malpractice insurance coverage, discussed below.

If you agree to perform a certain amount of work or to make a certain number of appearances or to handle certain specific cases in exchange for rent, this could be a great mutually-beneficial arrangement. Just don't allow un-used time to accumulate. Your obligation should expire at the end of each month, unless you agree to a short (say, one-month) carry-over period. You don't want to find yourself on the hook for more time than you can spare at a time when you really can't spare any.

Remember that your spare time may soon become scarce. Limit your obligations to allow the growth of your practice. The attorneys offering the space-for-time will probably be glad to get *any* value from the unproductive office space you will occupy, so their demands on your time may not be great. You, on the other hand, will need every hour you can muster. Value your time accordingly. If you sell yourself too cheaply in the beginning, it will be hard later on to set it straight. If you ask for too much, you can always come down.

These arrangements can become complicated, so it is necessary to put all of the terms in writing. Be precise. New attorneys are sometimes reluctant to propose to older lawyers that their agreement be reduced to writing. Have no fear; bring up the subject early on. Then YOU prepare the first draft, if they'll let you. If not, review their draft and be prepared to make suggestions and raise objections to their draft. There may be a lot of back-and-forth on minor matters, or there may be none at all. In either case, a comprehensive written understanding will avoid conflict later on.

They Don't Teach You THIS in Law School

Sending a Thank You note is the best way to get people to remember you favorably after you've had a pleasant interaction. It is extremely effective at building relationships. Handwritten is better than email, and an interesting postage stamp completes the package.

The "thankee" may forget having done you a favor; the personal note keeps the connection alive.

Cooperative Office Arrangements

An increasingly popular set-up is the cooperative office, where independent lawyers or small partnerships work alongside each other and share office amenities. Often, though not always, these are offices in professional buildings in which one attorney or firm has an ownership interest or master lease, and there is extra office space available. Big firms that have down-sized have plenty of such space, in some markets. The firm rents out private professional offices within its suite or building to unaffiliated lawyers, each of whom pays the landlord a monthly fee in exchange for an office space, receptionist, conference room, law library, and access to certain office equipment. The landlord will probably make vague promises of maybe referring you some overflow work or conflicts. Don't count on oral assurances of work.

Sometimes, each of the attorneys in these arrangements has her own separate full-time secretarial and administrative personnel. Sometimes each hires his own part-time people. Often, they join forces and hire a full time person, whose services they share. Sometimes they agree to pay the landlord for the use of her secretarial or administrative staff, which is generally billed on an hourly basis and added to the rent bill. In the right circumstances, this kind of office is excellent for a new solo.

Ideally, the individual lawyers in such a situation would have diverse specialties or preferences to allow for synergy and referrals among themselves. "Healthy competition" among suitemates does not usually survive in this environment. Peaceful co-existence might. Synergy works best.

> **"New attorneys are reluctant to propose to older lawyers that their agreement be reduced to writing. Have no fear; bring up the subject early on."**

Like law firms, these offices have their own personalities. In some, the lawyers see each other frequently, go out to lunch with each other, socialize after hours, and spread business around the suite when they can. They enjoy a true sense of camaraderie. In others suites, they walk unseeingly past the receptionist in the morning and have little to do with each other during the course of the week. Lawyers who travel frequently may only need the office as a *pied-a-terre*, or base of operations, from time to remote time. Their offices may be empty almost all the time. Perhaps that ounds just fine for you. Perhaps that is not at all what you are looking for.

"Business Centers" and "Professional Suites"

Similar to office-sharing in a legal suite are the cooperative offices where, for one monthly fee, individual businesses or professionals share a prestigious address, professional receptionist, access to a common conference room and certain amenities. Each tenant has a private office or offices, according to need. This sort of arrangement is rapidly increasing in popularity, as lawyers look to provide a high level of professionalism and service to clients, while keeping costs low.

Certain real estate investment and management companies specialize in providing these suites. One such company is Regus, which operates Regus Business Centers in cities around the world. Their properties tend to be in busy commercial areas, on major highways and in office complexes. They are generally very nice offices which do not suggest that you are just getting started. You may have a contract to rent the space for as few as a handful of days per year, or a set number of days per week. The rent is considerable, but the properties are usually first class, and amenities abound.

One of the advantages is that these arrangements often require only a short-term obligation. Unlike commercial leaseholds, which may run for five or ten years or more, your office sharing arrangement should keep your exposure to a minimum. Your first year or two may bring success or new opportunities. It may also lead you on a different path. In either case, you should not join a sharing arrangement that requires a long-term commitment. One disadvantage is that tend to be very expensive, especially when the landlord is a major player in that market and offers only prime properties. You may not need such luxury.

Look for other individual building owners and property management firms offering these arrangements, perhaps a step or two less luxurious but far less costly.. You should be able to find them with some basic internet research. Visit the property *before* your appointment and chat up one of the tenants. Someone will speak to you frankly about the arrangement and the landlord.

These business centers or suites often include not only lawyers, but diverse businesses and professionals. For some lawyers, this is seen as a plus. They prefer to not work around other lawyers. Besides, as the only lawyer in the suite, it may be tempting to think of yourself as ultimately representing your non-attorney suite-mates in their legal matters. Of course, this is possible. However, while you may get some business by being the only lawyer in the group, it is still better to share an office with lawyers only, if you can.

Not only is it helpful to have other legal minds with which to brainstorm and to offer other perspectives, but you may have access to the other lawyers' "overflow" or conflict matters, and you may be able to "cover" for each other as the need arises. Lawyers remain the single best source of business for other lawyers. Remember that. Other lawyers are your colleagues, not your competition. Treat them that way.

Going All Out (or "All In")

Maybe you have enough backing or enough "guaranteed" business to enable you to rent or buy office space of your own. Lucky you. There is probably abundant opportunity for you, considering the low office rents and the vast pool of office help that is available. By now, you have calculated the cost of renting or buying an office, and it just doesn't seem like too much money. If you can cater to a clientele that expects a fine office and is able to help you support it, this may be the best avenue.

Purchasing an office condo or securing a long-term lease for the office space you covet is the most ambitious way to go, and requires more than a minimum of economic staying power.

However, if you can afford it, and your plans allow for growth, your risk may yield handsome returns.

Location is often the most important factor in choosing your office. You will want your office to be convenient for you and for your clients while being close to the services you need. Of course, you should always have access to other attorneys for counsel. Ask them about the neighborhood, the other lawyers in the building or the area. Ask their advice. It is often not enough to discuss matters over the phone or internet with your mentors.   See if one will come with you to give his opinion. Even if you know the area around the office very well, learn whatever else you can. Discuss your thoughts with neighbors and other lawyers who might offer insight. You might even get leads to a better place.

Commercial leases are usually for a fixed amount of years, with the lease or rental amount usually described as the total for the contract period. The rent is then usually calculated monthly. Sometimes there are provisions for rental increases or increases triggered by specific events, such as an increase in the landlord's taxes or taking on a subtenant or lessee. It is a good to negotiate for an option to renew. This protects you and your investment in your practice and the goodwill you have established at that address.

> **"[N]egotiate for an option to renew. This protects you and your investment in your practice…"**

At some point, you will have to figure out what sort of initial term is most comfortable for you. Then, propose that term to the landlord and insist on an option to extend the agreement in the event that the arrangement is working out for you. Six months may be a good term for starters, although many landlords will object to any term of less than one year. Of course, with a glut of empty office space in many markets, landlords may agree to such a term. You won't know until you ask. Ask.

The amount of rent during the option period can always be left open and negotiated later, but bargain for the right to an option. This can be tricky. If your practice is doing well, you may wish to stay for a long time. A long-term lease will obligate you to pay a large amount of money, even if you are unable to continue in practice, or if rents drop in the area.

There is no ideal situation; a short-term lease has disadvantages as well. For example, a month-to-month situation or even year-to-year, may have the flexibility you seek, but it can also mean disaster if you are forced to move out against your will or at an inopportune moment. But you are a lawyer; you can figure these things out.

If your office space exceeds your present needs, hopefully it will accommodate your future growth. With some forethought, you may be able to turn your "too big" office into a productive asset immediately. If you have a say in designing the office layout, use all of your space wisely. Will you need a waiting room? If so, it should be comfortable and nicely furnished. However, if you almost never have people waiting, and your need for more space is acute, you will rue having a large waiting room. A similar thought process applies to a library, conference room, "break" room, kitchenette or other accessory use of space. Libraries, which are becoming obsolete, and conference rooms, are often combined.

If your private office is large enough, or if you don't expect conferences, depositions and meetings to exceed a limited number of people, consider having a small conference table in your personal office. This will prevent the dedication of valuable space to an infrequent use. Since you are anticipating growth, try to have at least one "extra" office available for eventual use by an associate, "counsel" to your firm, or for your paralegals and interns. Consider renting an extra office to other attorneys under such terms as the ones mentioned above, particularly attorneys who can bring business referrals or complementary skills to your office.

Having your own office is appealing, and may hasten your success. It may impress potential clients by giving you the semblance of being well-established. In the right location, it will even serve as a credential. If you are a Wall Street lawyer, for example, the perception is that you *must* be good. Each town has streets with addresses that suggest success. Do you want to be there? Do you *need* to be? You know best.

Your office can convey your personality or project an image you wish to cast. If your office is in an old carriage house, for example, or in a triangular room, or in a converted bank vault, you must be very cool. If you have a window office in a downtown building next to household-name lawyers, you must be expensive. Your office will speak for you, so choose it carefully.

Having your own office gives you control over the disposition, décor and ambiance of your work environment. You choose the person that answers your phone, the phone system itself, and the after-hours message. You choose the color of the walls and the background music that's playing. If you can afford to maintain your own office, you have an advantage from the start...maybe.

There are many obvious and not-so-obvious costs associated with this sort of independence. Heat and utilities, file cabinets, furniture, water coolers, fire extinguishers, municipal special assessment districts, PBA donations and your landlord's tax increases may all be among the expense of running a "real office." Many potential expenses are negotiable with the landlord. Negotiate *before* you move in.   If you expect to sign a long-term lease for an expensive office, use a commercial real estate agent to negotiate for you. They usually earn their fees.

> " **Most lease terms can be negotiable.**
> **In any event, there is no harm in asking.**"

If you are renting, prepare your ideal rental agreement as if you were doing it for a client. Review several commercial leases for terms and language that appeal to you. It won't take long to see that landlords' leases and tenants' leases are dramatically different from each other. Incorporate all favorable terms (your "wish list") into your proposed lease.

Be fair, but be fairer to yourself. Your landlord may tell you that *he* will prepare the lease, and that there is no room for modification. While that may be true, it rarely is. Most terms can be negotiable. In any event, there is no harm in asking. There is also no harm in asking other attorneys for input and suggestions. Develop the habit.

Opening a Satellite Office

It may seem pretentious. It may appear crazy. But sometimes, even for a new lawyer, it may make sense to have two offices. Usually, this happens when the lawyer draws business from two different jurisdictions. Perhaps he has lived in one and has worked in another. Perhaps he has an office in the county seat, and another in the heart of the minority neighborhood from which much business might flow. Perhaps one location accommodates a general practice, and the other feeds a specialty.

There are all sorts of reasons to have a second office. There are also reasons to NOT have one. Look at your circumstance, not your ego. Decide if it makes sense for you.

Typically, in a two-office scenario, your second office will be a room in another lawyer's office, or a bare bones affair that gives you an address at which you principally meet clients. Rarely will you need two fully-equipped offices. In the right circumstance, having a satellite office will allow you to schedule appointments with people who would otherwise find it inconvenient to work with you. One thing is sure: clients prefer a lawyer who's close to where they live or do business.

Having a convenient place to meet will sometimes make the difference between your getting a potential client and losing one. If you open a true satellite office, make sure that your card and letterhead and promotional material are in compliance with your bar's ethical standards, and remember to explain the circumstances to your insurers.

It may be easier and less expensive if you work out a mutually-beneficial arrangement with a lawyer or other person who has an extra office, to borrow that office from time to time, in order to meet with clients. Your volume of business will help you determine your approach.

They don't teach you THIS in Law School!

When opening your trust and business accounts, consider using two different banks. This will reduce the possibility of confusing your deposit, and will enable you to develop relationships with two sets of bankers.

III.

Start Small, Start Smart

You Need a Business Plan

It really doesn't matter. You may have potential clients waiting in the wings for you to represent them, or you may no idea where your clients will come from. You may have no real experience in any field of law, or you may have honed your expertise long before law school. You make seek a life of comfortable anonymity or the thrill of hobnobbing with the *glitterati*. Whatever your ambition, whatever your vision, one thing is sure: you will need a business plan.

There is no standard form of business plan for lawyers. You must define your mission and provide an explanation of your business's structure and function. It's really easy, but it still takes some clear thought.

A business plan does two things. First, it provides a picture of your business. How will it be structured? Will you be alone? Will you have an office? Two offices? Will you have employees? Part-timers? How will you get business? How will you get paid? How will you pay others? Will you specialize?

A business plan also provides a projection of your costs and revenue and growth. What will it cost to stay in business? Where will money come from? How long of a drought can you survive? How much can you reasonably expect to earn in a given period? Where will you be next year at this time? In five years? In ten years? Where do you want to be?

Creating a business plan will make you articulate your goals and reflect upon the soundness of your thinking. You should be able to say something like, "*I wish to practice out of a rented office in a suite with other lawyers. My practice will be general, at first, but I will solicit, and hope to specialize in matrimonial work, and maybe another specialty, such as adoptions. I expect to make appearances on routine matters, such as uncontested divorces, for other lawyers, and I will hold myself out to the public as a general practitioner with an emphasis on those matters. I expect to make about $1100 per week after a month or so, and perhaps $1,500 – 2,000 per week after eighteen months.*"

Projections of this type are typically unreliable, but, if they are at all realistic, they will serve as guideposts as you go along, demarcating the brink of success and the brink of disaster. This kind of business plan need not be formal. If you are able to prepare such a statement, you are well on the way to having your business plan. If you cannot, take the time to reflect on what you want. Then, create a plan that can get you there. There is one.

If you need to create a formal business plan to satisfy a bank or to solicit a grant, there is a wealth of free information in libraries and on the internet. Your law school placement or careers office will also be able to help you with your plan. Your law school might also put you in touch with attorneys whose practices resemble your model. They can be extraordinarily helpful. Also, check out the helpful "solo" websites mentioned earlier, such as "MyShingle," "SoloPracticeUniversity" and "SoloSez."

Sole Proprietor, P.A or LLP?

Some matters should be addressed immediately, because they are more easily handled at the outset of your mission than they will be later on. Such a matter is your business structure, the legal form you will give to your practice. In essence, you are a one-person business. You own everything that your practice owns. You must segregate your personal assets from those of your business. You should consider creating a corporate shield.

Even as a sole proprietor, it is probably a good idea to set up your practice as a corporation or an LLC or LLP (Limited Liability Corporation/Practice). All states allow some form of corporate protection to certain professional practices. Some states authorize entities call Professional Associations (P.A.). They all do the same thing.

For a new solo, there may be no tax advantages, but the corporate form may protect your personal assets in the event of unsatisfied creditors or a judgment against your practice. Also, in the event of a random audit, the corporate format will usually segregate your personal from your business affairs, where a Schedule C will not.

When you are ready to decide how your business should be organized, don't make that decision alone, even if you know what you want. Consult with at least one other lawyer and an accountant. If you don't already have a relationship with an accountant, this is a good time to develop one. Your best bet is a Certified Public Accountant, as they had to pass a very hard test, just as you did.

There are other low-cost sources of expertise that may be available. State bar associations usually have special sections or committees that serve solos and small practitioners. Contact the chair or visit their website. You will find information on setting up your business and getting it off the ground. Most of the legwork will be administrative minutia, such as registering the official name of your business, and making sure it is yours alone.

Do not delay in taking care of these tasks. Errors or delays in filing your paperwork with the bar or in publishing "fictitious business name notices" in newspapers may create problems with your bank, with the bar, and with other administrative aspects of your start-up. Talk first to a lawyer who has recently done it. You can find one.

You may also qualify as a "minority owned" or "woman owned" business, if you meet the criteria. Various governmental programs in many states and some cities make generous provisions to assist historically underrepresented ownership groups. Often, benefits include subsidized business loans, favorable tax treatment, and advantageous positioning bidding on government contracts. If you may qualify, look into what is available.

Why Not a Partnership?

This book is not written exclusively for young lawyers who wish to be solos. The information should be equally valid for partnerships. New attorneys striking out on their own may be attracted to the idea of partnership, often with another new attorney or two. They may see such synergy between their interests and abilities that they feel drawn into a natural partnership or they want to partner up to avoid the feeling of drifting alone at sea. It is understandable, but dangerous.

Some attorneys believe that there is no such thing as a good partnership. But, of course, each case is unique. Evaluate each opportunity on its own merit, but remember, partnerships are like marriages; they all start off rosy with dreams of success. How they end is often ugly, costly and counterproductive.

It is probably a good idea to see how you work on your own before you throw your hat into the ring with others.

> **"Some attorneys believe that there is no such thing as a good partnership."**

A tempting scenario for partnership sometimes arises when a young attorney starts working with an established solo or partnership. You may find yourself associating with an older lawyer or with a retiring attorney looking for someone to continue the practice for any number of reasons. You may consider forming a partnership to achieve mutual goals. Before you do that, examine other ways than partnership to enjoy the benefits of experienced counsel and professional synergy, even as a solo.

Partnerships rarely end up with workload and income distributed among partners 50-50 or 33-33-33. In most cases, each partner feels that she is doing more than the others, or is inadequately compensated, or is "carrying" another partner. There is often more friction than synergy between partners. What starts as friendly chiding between partners may reveal a rift that only grows. If business is slow, partners suffer together. If business is good, they often break up. But, of course there are some advantages to partnership.

Fortunately, most of the advantages of partnership can be attained by solos through intelligent relationships. You and your would-be partners can set up parallel solo practices, form strategic alliances with each other, and see how it goes. In time, maybe you can form some permanent entity, but in the beginning, focus your assets and efforts at launching your career.

Partners waste time and money disagreeing over items that solos never consider, such as whose name goes first on the letterhead or who gets the smaller office, or who originated the client. A busy solo should have no time or energy to devote to such matters.

Furniture and Equipment

Irrespective of the type of practice you build, and notwithstanding the various sorts of office arrangements to consider, you will need some specific material and equipment in order to get started. Some of these, such as file cabinets and desks, involve one-time expenses. Others, like your insurances and lease payments on a high-volume photocopier, are payable at regular intervals. Still others, such as replacement cartridges for your printer, or equipment repair, involve periodic or unexpected expenses. When it comes to expenses, learn to expect the unexpected.

Whatever your practice, however you pay your rent, getting the office space is just the beginning. You will need to spend some money to set up a basic office. Sit down with a few solos and discuss their practices. Ask them about their expenses. Listen carefully to their list of usual and extraordinary costs of doing business. Is *your* list realistic? Can you afford what you will need? Will you have enough money left over?

> **"When it comes to expenses, expect the unexpected."**

Generally, you will need desks and chairs. You should have a telephone system and a computer with internet access. Your "smart phone" will probably not suffice. In most states, you will need a dedicated business phone number in order to be listed in phone directories and other professional listings. Moreover, you are not an ordinary business person...you are a lawyer. You are obligated to treat your clientele with a certain level of professionalism. That level is not met when you do not have a business phone. Get one with caller ID. You'll be very glad you did.

It is helpful to have a memorable or catchy phone number. These generally have several zeros, pairs of numbers, or other features that make them easier to remember. Most phone company representatives will try to help you find a special number, if you ask them.

You will also need a computer. If you are relying on your PC or laptop to serve your business and personal needs, take measures to segregate your business and personal files and to secure your computer against unauthorized use and accidental exposure of confidential files. For similar reasons, keep a business email address that is separate from your personal email addresses.

You will probably need a file cabinet or two. Although the world is moving toward digital files, lawyers still need to store paper. Paper files are best kept in heavy-duty file folders and classified in a heavy duty file cabinet. If you will be routinely storing valuable documents, you should consider a fire-resistant cabinet. For most uses, a regular legal size office file cabinet should suffice. These should be readily available on the second-hand market. Try out various systems. You may prefer cabinets in which the files face forward rather than sideways or a system that features "suspension" drawers which facilitate opening and closing. They are more expensive, but they may well be worth the difference.

You will need a good quality photocopy machine, fax and printer. If your practice does not seem to demand much copying, you might be able to rely on your printer or a printer/scanner/fax to do your work. Your vision of your practice should help you decide upon the size, capacity and features of the machines. Estimate how heavy your use will be, and get a machine that is sufficient for your needs.

The copier is most important. Will you require color printing often enough to justify the expense? Do you need laser, or will ink-jet do? Will you require automatic two-sided copying? Will you need collation of multi-page documents or an automatic stapling device?

The two significant expenses associated with copiers and printers are maintenance contracts and toner or ink. Find out from independent sources how many copies you will get from a cartridge, and how much each cartridge costs. Ask how much a maintenance agreement will be, and whether routine maintenance is free. Find out what routine maintenance means.

Many small offices "lease to buy" their equipment. They pay a low monthly charge for two or three or four or five years, at the end of which time they can buy it outright at a pre-set price or according to a formula. Often, the lease includes service components, such as free checkups, and no-fee routine maintenance. If you buy the equipment at lease-end, you will probably still want to purchase a maintenance contract going forward. These are expensive, particularly for older equipment. Try to figure the cost of a few service visits per year. Usually, the contract makes economic sense.

A facsimile machine (fax) is also essential. You may wish to own your fax machine before you order your stationery, since the fax number should appear on your card and your letterhead.

Often, fax machines are combined with a scanner, copier, phone, and printer into a device called a "multi-function," "four-in-one" or a "five-in-one" machine. If your paperwork load is minimal, such a unit may fill your needs, at least temporarily. Beware, however that these are generally regarded as consumer products, meaning that they are meant for home-office or small-office use; they are usually not heavy-duty or particularly durable pieces of equipment. Also, the printer toner is usually contained in smaller cartridges which are more costly and require more frequent replacement than the heavier-duty machines intended for offices. Shop carefully.

Stationery and Supplies

You will also need business cards, stationery (including letterhead), and some standard office forms. Your business card is very important. It should be dignified and easy to read. It should look like a lawyer's card. As a young lawyer, you may have enough trouble proving your merit. Your business card should not be shocking or cheap-looking. It must be one you are proud of.

Of course, within limits set by your bar, you may put promotional information on the card. You may include state bar admissions, professional specialties, board certification, additional degrees and addresses, and similar matter, provided you do not run afoul of your bar's advertising rules.

Do not count on your printing company, even a legal printer, to know the rules. Confirm that your card is "street legal" before you go to press. An ounce of prevention...

Even today, with electronic mail and e-filing of papers, every lawyer needs a letterhead for correspondence. Your stationery is often the first impression a potential client (or an adversary) will have of you and your practice.

You will need, at the very least, letterhead and envelopes. With a computer on every desk, these days, more and more attorneys are abandoning printed letterhead in favor of computer-generated forms. Your letterhead and business card should have the same typeface, or "look." This is one minor way to "brand" yourself. Some attorneys agonize more over the design of their letterhead and business cards than any other aspect of the start-up. That is easy to understand.

Computer-generated "stationery" is adequate for many purposes, but to create the best impression, a quality printed letterhead on good paper is best. For your "demand letters" and correspondence with adversaries, judges and clients, for letters seeking *per diem* work with other lawyers, and whenever else it is important to set your best foot forward, you should use your best stationery. For routine cover letters and correspondence with clerks and administrators, computer-generated letterhead may be economical and efficient. Use your judgment, but keep some "fancy" letterhead handy.

If you plan on having a new domain name or website, a new email address or any similar change, hold up on printing your letterhead until you have the permanent information you will need.

At the time you order your letterhead, you may consider buying "return envelopes." These are cut a bit smaller than the standard #10 envelopes so they can fit inside, and imprinted with your name and address as addressee. They are helpful in getting people to mail papers, such as signed documents or checks, back to you. Courts also require that you send them, stamped, when sending in papers for filing. Depending on the nature of the work you are doing, you may find these self-addressed envelopes essential or superfluous.

A great invention is the tear-apart NCR ("no carbon required") form for memos. These are one-page memos which can be time-saving if you just want to jot off a quick note, such as confirming an appointment or an understanding or saying thank you. It automatically produces one or two copies, depending on the style you buy. You write the recipient's address in the correct spot, and it appears as the address through a window envelope designed accordingly and imprinted with your return address. These can be very helpful in a variety of ways. If they are not too expensive for you, they can save more than just your time. They just may save your rear.

If you prepare Wills, you may wish to print your name and address on printed Last Will and Testament cover pages and envelopes. These are elegant, high-quality supplies available through legal printing houses. They are a bit pricey, but are far more impressive than any other system. They will pay for themselves with the first Will you do.

More and more attorneys, even old-timers, are spitting out simple Wills on cheap letter-size copy paper direct from their ink jet printer. Such an important document, which may last 50 or 60 years or more after signing, should always be on durable paper. High-quality printed Will forms show your concern for quality and suggest excellence.

In addition to forms and stationery, you will need a slew of office supplies, including Scotch tape, scissors, staplers, staples, and staple removers, pads, pens, pencils, pencil sharpener, paper, paper clips and paper punches. You may need rubber stamps, binder clamps and reading lamps. Buy wisely, and don't get carried away. You can always go back to the store.

They don't teach you THIS in Law School!

When stapling papers together, always staple at a 45-degree angle from the top and side. If the staple is parallel to a side, it will soon tear the paper when the sheets are folded back. Stapling at a neat 45 anticipates the fold, and the staple, properly placed, will hold forever.

Secretaries, Paralegals, Law Clerks and Legal Interns

Every self-employed lawyer recognizes the importance of getting new business. Equally important is getting the work done. Most lawyers rely on secretaries, paralegals, clerks or interns to do this. In the beginning, you may be your own secretarial staff. Depending on your competence and the nature of your practice, you may continue this way for years.

Some solo attorneys, handy with keyboards and office methods, have completely eliminated support staff. If you can cut-and-paste your way through your paperwork without the assistance of others, you may avoid great expense over time. It is important, however to recognize the point at which it becomes counterproductive to continue as your own support staff. You will reach a point when your time is better spent doing lawyer-work or client development.

In some practices areas, much, if not most, of the work is clerical and is typically done by law clerks, paralegals or secretaries. With a competent staff, the caseload requires little handling by an attorney. Paralegals are available on a part-time or full time basis. Efficient use of staff may allow you to grow from the beginning. Immigration, foreclosures, collections, appeals of insurance denials, and residential real estate are paralegal-intensive fields. The attorney gets involved in negotiation and advising the client, and will appear in court or at the closing of a deal, but the time-consuming work is done by staff.

Employing part-timers will let you bridge the gap to a full-time person or staff. Your staff should be your most valuable asset, so select them carefully. Remember that your staff may also become your greatest single cost, so be conservative in what you pay and what terms you can afford to offer. When hiring a secretary, try to find one with legal experience. Check his credentials. Find out what he knows.

If you have a specialty, or would like to develop one, look for staff with that experience in that specialty. If you just need a typist, there are many typing and transcription services available. They are usually cost-effective, but do not expect a typist to understand procedural requirements, to know your various court deadlines or to figure out that you forgot to dictate an affidavit, unless you hire a more expensive legal secretary or legal typist.

Choose your people carefully. As a general rule, the less experienced you are, the more experienced your staff should be. Yet, no matter how competent your staff is, you must still take the time to know how to do their jobs. You are the attorney; the buck stops with you. If your secretary or paralegal makes an error with filing a paper or preparing a document, you should be able to spot it and know how to fix it.

If your practice involves court, learn the Rules of Court. Read them all. Learn all you can about filing briefs and motions and other papers. Learn how to prepare a caption page for pleadings, and memorize the time limits for discovery procedures. You will be a better lawyer when you know what's in the Rules.

Paralegals have a general education in the principal fields of law, and work for lawyers, usually in a legal specialty. Their abilities may run from awful to awesome. In some states, most anyone can call himself a paralegal; in others, paralegal training is required and state certification is issued only upon successful fulfillment of state-sanctioned requirements.

Some law firms employ more paralegals than lawyers, and the trend is growing. While paralegals still cannot appear in court, they can do almost anything else that lawyers do, under the auspices of an attorney. Paralegals commonly review and draft routine documents and correspondence, organize litigation files, generate discovery, summarize depositions, fill in forms, meet with clients and prepare legal research. The more specialized the practice, the more specialized will be the paralegal's knowledge and ability. A top-quality, self-starting paralegal will not be inexpensive, but may prove to be invaluable.

Law clerks are usually law students who work a few hours per week. Properly utilized, they can be a great bargain. Posting an ad at a nearby law school or in the legal newspaper will usually bring a sufficient pool of applicants. Law clerks principally perform legal research and prepare legal documents. They may work from their home or out of your office. You may hire them on a regular schedule or on an "as needed" or "per project" basis. They should be closely supervised, as you will be their mentor and guide, in addition to being their employer. Law clerks go on to become lawyers, and many former law clerks have gone on to bring their former employers some excellent clients and lucrative cases.

A relatively new arrival on the scene is the "legal intern." Legal interns are usually law students with more interest than experience, who will work for little or no money. Paid or unpaid, they want the experience or credential of working in a law office, and they will generally do whatever they are asked. Internships are often arranged through local law schools, although firms may certainly offer them on their own, if they do not conflict with labor laws. The employer is required to spend a certain amount of time providing instruction to his minions.

> **"Law clerks are law students who work a few hours per week. Properly utilized, they can be a great bargain."**

Like law clerks, legal interns may be a great asset, but the biggest problem may be keeping them busy for the required amount of time, or providing guidance to them when your own learning curve is so steep. Legal interns may be better suited for larger firms that have more extensive needs and several lawyers to share the task-giving and the tutoring. All things considered, law clerks remain the better bargain.

Filing Systems

You will need a system for organizing and storing your files. If you set up a sensible system at the beginning, you will avoid problems later on. Your system should include some sort of digital (computerized) file containing your case and client information for each new matter you open. You should also keep a separate card with that information for each new client or matter. This will serve as a backup and will assist you in finding files or client information in the future.   Ask other lawyers about the systems they use and why they like or dislike them.

You should have standard intake forms that you use for opening a file. Do not open a file without one. This will prevent you from omitting important information. Different types of files will require different information on intake.   Don't just rely on someone else's form. Develop one you like.

In all cases, however, certain basic information must be obtained.   Include the client's name and address and phone number(s). Indicate the preferred phone number or best mailing address. Other attorneys will gladly let you "borrow" the intake forms they have developed. The form should include space for the client's name(s), date of birth and social security number (to confirm identity later on, to help complete forms, or to provide information to insurance carriers paying injury claims). It should note the type of case it is. It should contain contact numbers and other relevant client data.

If the case is a lawsuit, your client's name should come first, even if he is the defendant. If you represent John Doe who is suing Jane Roe, the case is *Doe v. Roe*. However, if Roe is suing your client, the case is *Doe adv. Roe*, in your file.

You will need to separate active files from closed files. Still, there will be some matters you will wish to keep handy long after your file is officially closed. Certain matters such as Wills or Trusts should never be closed, until, at least, there has been a final official accounting of the matter. For this reason, you may decide to have a separate file drawer, and perhaps a separate filing system, for Wills and Trusts.

Corporate formations also may be long-lived files. For this, and other, reasons, if you handle corporate set-ups, recommend that your client keep the corporate book and seal and certificates. Unless the corporation has active corporate business for you, don't keep the original books and records. The great majority of corporations you will form will not ask for the paperwork after six months following formation. Don't saddle yourself with the responsibility of being custodian of the records, however nice the corporate books look on your bookshelf, unless that role portends business for you later on.

Your filing systems should facilitate your future retrieval of a file. Your computerized filing system should be able to sort your matter by case type, client name, and date of event. You may even be able to punch in a source's name and retrieve the names of all cases s/he sent you.

For "hard" files, you can color code the file jackets and client cards. This can come in handy when you are looking for an old file but can't remember the client's name, or if you wish to search a certain type of file for work you've done or for forms you've created or used.

Many lawyers use two filing systems for each case – an alphabetical system for files that are open, and a numerical system for closed files. Where you have multiple open files for a single client, you can assign to each file a secondary name, such as a description of the type of matter, or the name of an adverse party. The filing of mail and phone memos and conflict-identification are made easy with an alphabetical filing system.

On the other hand, it makes sense to use a numerical system for filing *closed* files. They pile up quickly and should be enumerated in the order that they are closed.   Imagine filing closed files alphabetically, and having to squeeze Mr. Lee's four "red rope" expanding files into a drawer full of "L" files. Numerical filing of closed files will also facilitate retrieving those files years later, when you no longer recognize the client or the case.

Client Cards

When you open a file, put the essential client information on a separately filed permanent card you may call a client card. You may even note certain additional information on the file jacket, such as the name of the "forwarder," or source of the business (e.g., John Jones, Esq., website, Aunt Mary).   Not only does this help you remember where your business comes from, it also facilitates your sending thank you notes.

Do not assume that you will remember who sent you all of your clients. In time, you will lose track. Keeping the information readily available will often be helpful. You may also wish your client card to include family information such as spouse's and children's names, hobbies, house of worship, languages spoken and other personal information.

> **"Be careful that ...confidential client information is not visible on the file jacket."**

Many lawyers use printed labels for their file folders. These are available at most legal printers and supply houses. Sometimes, these labels are part of a popular multi-page carbonized system that, at the time you open your file, creates a 3x5 in. file card and two or three 3x5 in. colored labels simultaneously. Affix one label to your file jacket. Be careful that the intake information or any other confidential client information is not visible on the file jacket. Addresses, birthdates, forwarders' names, and social security numbers have no business being where they can be seen by others.

When you close the file, mark the permanent card with the closed file number you assigned, or otherwise indicate the location of the file. When, after years, you destroy the file, you will note that information on the file card, too. When clients call you to report address changes or want you to have their new cell phone numbers, put that information on the client's permanent card, right away. You never know when you'll need it.

Your Diary

Your diary is a very important part of your daily life. With good diary habits, you will save yourself stress and inconvenience. If you cannot maintain a complete and constantly-changing diary, don't try being a solo lawyer.

Your diary serves three principal functions.

1. Appointments and Appearances

Your professional life will center on your appointments. A lawyer cannot overstate the value of a reliable, accessible calendar or diary. It is a good idea to keep one calendar in your office and one on your person. One calendar may be electronic, but at least one should be paper. Coordinate the two at the end of each day. The important thing is to have your appointments in order. Often, in court, a judge will offer you the courtesy of setting a hearing date that is convenient to you. It will sound like, *"How's December 16, counsel?"* If you have your diary handy, you will know whether that date works for you. If you are unprepared, the judge will set that date, leaving you to try to get out of it later on, when you learn that you have a conflict.

Appointments include meetings, luncheons, haircuts, dental and medical visits, errands and social events. They can be very important. Your most important calendar events, however, will be your court appearances. Your diary should contain all of your court appearances, hearings, discovery proceedings, and conferences. If your client's attendance is required, and it usually will be, you should not assume that your client's diary is as reliable as yours.

It is always a good idea to notify, or remind your clients *in writing,* of court dates and other appearances. Send your clients a letter or email stating that they should call you to confirm, the day before the scheduled event. If they do not call, you should call your clients to make sure they will be there. You will often be glad that you did.

When you have a court appearance scheduled, you should always confirm the appearance the day before (or on Friday before a Monday appearance). You will be surprised at how many appearances will be rescheduled without your knowledge. Instruct your clients to notify you if they learn of any changes, and you should tell your clients when you hear of any changes. Do not assume that, just because your copy of the court notice says that your client was also sent a notice, it actually happened. The same is true of depositions and other events requiring your clients' attendance. Confirm such dates in writing whenever possible.

2. Deadlines and Ticklers

In addition to appointments that must be diaried, lawyers usually have deadlines. Litigation, real estate, commercial work, immigration, criminal defense and many other fields of law are deadline-intensive. Again, you will need a good system. This can be combined with your appointments and appearances or kept in a separate calendar. Using the same diary, you can enter appointments and appearances in pencil (since they change frequently) and enter deadlines in colored ink. You should review your appointments at least daily and your deadlines at least twice a week.

Develop a routine for inserting "ticklers." The electronic age has made this practically effortless. Ticklers are reminders that an important date is approaching. For certain matters, you may want a 30-day tickler. For others, a day or two is adequate. Establish a protocol for entering ticklers whenever you make a diary entry that will require your attention in advance.

For example, if you enter an event such as someone's birthday, you may wish to enter a tickler a few days in advance to remind you to order a birthday cake, or to buy a card. If you must have a brief done by a certain date, that date will certainly be entered in your "deadlines" diary. But you may also want to tickle yourself with a date by which to finish your research or the last day you can send the brief to the printer for binding.

3. Return Mail File

Similar to ticklers is the "return mail file." This diary notation lets you keep track of deadlines you have set for others. For example, you may tell an adverse party, "If I don't hear from you by August 3, we will..." or you may tell your client, "Please return the completed form to me by..." These reminders will enable you to handle matters with no undue delay.

Be careful when you send a deadline or ultimatum to your adversary, with a copy to your client.   Make sure the client understands in advance that there may not be immediate execution of the threat. Do not send that letter unless you are prepared to meet your own deadline.   Clients won't understand the attorney who threatens the other side with action, and then, at the moment of truth, do nothing. They think: *"You promised action. You even got tough in that letter.   You gave them an ultimatum! A deadline! It came and went, and now you tell me I'll have to wait another week for any action by you?"*

Lawyers may understand that there is no rush.   They may realize that the letter is a bluff or a tactic or that the system is backed up for three months, or that everyone knows they will be able to vacate whatever you do, as soon as their lawyer steps in. Lawyers know that, but clients do not. Even though the delay may cost your client nothing, she still might not understand.

On the positive side, taking care of matters as they come up on your return mail file can enhance your reputation for diligence. People notice. If you handle the little matters promptly and return phone calls, you will gain a reputation for excellence and give people reasons to say nice things about you.

Form Files

Whether or not you expect your work to become repetitive, you should keep a "form file." The digital revolution has made this amazingly simple to do. A form file is a paper or digital folder containing any work that you've done, and any forms you have received or created, which may come in handy in the future. Standard forms, court-mandated forms, your personalized forms, form letters to clients and courts, and similar documents should be located where you can find them for use as a template or for guidance.

A form has little value if you can't find it when you need it. To aid retrieval, file your forms under multiple headings where appropriate. For example, a cover letter for filing a mortgage with the county clerk may be filed under "Real Estate Forms", "Mortgage Forms", and "Cover Letters." Save it under the client's name, too, if you wish. Many times you will think, *"I did something like this for old Hendershot, once."* File your form under "Hendershot," too. From time to time, you should cull and update your forms.

The time-saving advantage of a form file is obvious. One of the surprise advantages is that it can prove to be a business-builder. Often you will hear or overhear attorneys asking about finding a court form or preparing a routine-type paper. If you think it may be helpful, offer to send *your* form to that lawyer. In an instant you will have established yourself as someone with experience and tools and a willingness to share. That will set you apart from so many others. It could also be the beginning of a mutually-beneficial professional relationship. Exchange business cards and then send the form you promised without delay.

Malpractice Insurance

We all try to do the best work we can. However, we sometimes make mistakes and errors in judgment that can be costly to other people.   There is insurance, albeit expensive in certain specialties, to protect lawyers against that risk. Don't take chances. If you plan to sell your legal services to the public, you will almost certainly need to have Professional Errors and Omissions insurance.

> "If you plan to sell your legal services to the public, you will almost certainly need to have E & O insurance."

There are some exceptions to the rule that you must have malpractice insurance. If you are doing work for the legal department of a business, the company itself or the in-house lawyers you work for may have a business or umbrella policy or a malpractice policy that covers you. Find out.

If you are working under the auspices of another lawyer under any circumstances, make sure that all the work you perform for that office will be covered. Consider whether you might someday have exposure for negligence to the attorney's client, or even to the attorney you work for.

Do not assume that you are covered by the policy of the attorneys who give you assignments. Advise them in writing that you are uninsured and will only proceed if they assure you that you fall under their coverage.

If you are accepting "pool work" from various courts and state agencies, you may be "covered" for your representation of clients they provide. On the other hand, they may require *you* to have certain coverage before you can take their cases.

Before you buy legal malpractice insurance, you will need to do some basic research. Do not rely on insurance sales people to compare the apples and oranges for you, without looking into the policy options yourself. Check the available coverage, terms and premiums. They may vary widely. Where a choice of policy types is available, consider the advantages of a policy that provides coverage in a "claims made" basis. This means that there will be coverage for all claims made during the policy period, even if the event arose before. Of course, the application will require disclosure of any potential claims you are aware of. If you misrepresent this on your application, the carrier may, years later, seek to deny you coverage on a claim.

The amount of insurance you will need depends, not so much upon the likelihood of your being sued, but on the maximum amount you are likely to get sued for. This is largely a function of the types of cases you handle. If you plan to do transactional work, matrimonial cases, trust and estate work or litigation, you should be prepared to pay an expensive premium. If you limit your practice to criminal law, administrative law, municipal court or appellate work, your premiums should be markedly smaller.

If you intend to join referral panels or professional networks, ask about the minimum insurance coverage they require of their members. Before you sign for any malpractice coverage, check with your bar association, local attorneys, and consumer ratings services about the company or policy that interests you. Generally speaking, you should purchase this kind of coverage directly from an agent specializing in selling such insurance. Your bar association may have rating information for all qualified carriers in the state. Shop carefully. Rates vary widely, as do policy provisions.

> **"Your greatest source of trouble will almost always be the client, and it may not be the client's fault."**

Having malpractice insurance does not remove the burden of practicing defensively. Although you need not view each case as a potential lawsuit and each client as a potential plaintiff, you must be aware of the danger zones and the blind spots that we lawyers have. Deadlines are everywhere; adversaries abound. Conflicts of interest lurk in the bushes.

Still, your greatest source of trouble will almost always be the client, and it may not be the client's fault. Make sure that your personal traits - a quick temper, a lazy streak, a sharp tongue - do not translate into errors with files or issues with clients. You can do more than anyone to prevent claims against you by maintaining good relations with your clients.

Business Insurance

"Business insurance" is a term that encompasses all sorts of insurance against all sorts of risks. As a new solo, you normall will have rather limited needs. Discuss your insurance situation with a competent agent who will understand what you need.

Certainly, if you are inviting the public into your premises, you will need liability coverage. You buy most insurance (life, disability, fire) because of what it may pay *you*. Liability insurance is insurance that protects you by paying *others*. In the event that plaster from your bathroom ceiling lands on a client's head, or the letter carrier slips, trips, or otherwise falls in or around your office, you won't have to worry about losing your shirt. In some parts of the country, a policy of not less than $500,000 is usually appropriate, and in some areas, $1,000,000 of liability coverage is considered a minimum. Your agent should have a pretty good idea of what you'll need. Liability rates are very low for law offices.

Business insurance may contain "business interruption" or "business continuation" coverage. This assures you of continued income in the event your business is forced to close, or partly close, as a result of specified hazards such as fire and flood. That provision, or another, may pay off your rent obligation if you are unable to do so.

If your practice has employees, you may need workers' compensation insurance. "Comp" is usually separate from the other policies, but certain companies include workers' compensation coverage in their usual business insurance package. Generally, there are relatively few insurers serving this market, and a small handful has the lion's share of the market.

If you work from home, you may only require a "home office" endorsement on your homeowner's or renter's insurance policy. If you own the home, you may be able to reduce the premium on your business policy by tying it in with an "umbrella" policy on your home. It works like this: you would already have, say a $1,000,000 limit liability policy on your home. You would pay a bit more for an "umbrella" policy in that amount. Then, if you buy your business insurance from them, they will only require you to buy a $250,000 policy, with the agreement that, if you are sued, the umbrella coverage will kick in for up to $750,000 if your $250,000 has been exhausted. A similar arrangement may available for your automobile insurance. Speak to a reputable agent. Speak to a few. Rates vary significantly.

All homeowners seem to know that they need homeowners' insurance. People who rent often don't think about coverage. Renters' insurance is like homeowners' insurance for renters. If you are renting your house or apartment, and you don't have renters' insurance, get it immediately. In the event of a fire, flood or similar catastrophe, the owner's hazard insurance will not cover your loss. Renters' insurance is inexpensive and it is essential, even if you do not have an office in your home.

Dealing with reputable insurance companies is more important than saving a small amount on the premium. When you need to talk to an agent, you usually require prompt, reliable service. Web-based insurers cannot perform the same way that your friendly local professional can, assuming you have an accessible friendly local professional near to where you practice. Moreover, the insurance website will never send you any business, but your personal insurance agent might. Unless your options are strictly limited, purchase your insurance through a top local agent.

Disability Insurance

It may also be a good time to consider disability insurance. There are policies that will pay you regularly in the event that you are disabled from practicing. Bear in mind that the most common cause of disability among lawyers are stress and stress-related ailments. It is most important to choose a company that lets you define your profession specifically. Ask each representative how it works: If you are accepted as a "trial lawyer," for example, and a condition makes you unable to try cases, ask whether you will qualify for benefits, even though you might be able to practice some other legal specialty, say collections, with that disability. If you are assured of a favorable definition of disability, confirm it writing to the company or agent, before paying for the policy.

Your biggest obstacle as a novice attorney may be establishing an income history on which to base your request for disability coverage. Insurance companies handle this variously, and your agent should be able to help you satisfy these requirements. Many state bar associations have arrangements with insurers to provide supplemental disability income coverage to its members. These policies often have significant restrictions, but they may be low cost and worth considering when you sit down to figure out your insurances.

They Don't Teach You THIS in Law School

Keep track of your "referrers," the people who send you business. You may do this in several ways.

Keep a separate list of the names and addresses of each person who sends you a case. Then, at the time that you open the file, send a note of thanks to the source. Discreetly note the file with referrer's name. This way, when you are with the client, you may ask, *"How are Alan and Marie?"*

Or if the client says, *"Tom says, 'Hello,'"* you may avoid the awkwardness of asking, *"Tom who?"*

Banking – Business and Trust Accounts

You will need a bank, perhaps more than one. Choose a bank that is well-reputed and well-managed. Large national banks may be convenient, although for small practices, local and state banks are usually sufficient. You should develop a relationship with a banker. This may prove helpful in any number of ways. A friendly banker will keep a door open a few extra minutes if you are running late, or stall the payment of a check until your uncollected funds come through.

Bankers also usually know a lot of people, and can be excellent sources of referrals. You should look for a bank that can provide all the services you might need. You may not need anything more than a simple business account, but your clients may have more sophisticated banking needs. If you can bring your clients to your bank for the special accounts and services they offer, your banker may go out of her way to promote your practice.

Most solo practices need two bank accounts: a business account and a trust account. In some states, banks must have a special arrangement with the bar in order to offer attorney trust accounts. They must comply with special reporting and regulatory requirements that do not apply to any other type of account.

> **"Your attorney trust account is sacrosanct...**
> **One rule is invariable: the money in it is not yours."**

Many states have legal guidelines for the way that information must appear on attorneys' checks, particularly trust checks. Do not rely on some national bank to supply checks that conform to your state's requirements. Get a sample of the check and make sure that it conforms.

Your attorney trust account is sacrosanct. Whether you have many transaction and numerous checks passing through the account or the account is a rarely used in your practice, one rule is invariable: the money in it is not yours. If any part of the trust account is comingled with your personal funds or taken out wrongfully, not only may you suffer ethical sanctions, including loss of your license, but you may have criminal exposure as well.

All state bars have the power to review your trust accounts. Even if you handle all your other accounting, you may consider employing a bookkeeper or accountant to reconcile your trust account. Random audits and targeted audits reveal that many attorneys are far more casual than they should be their trust accounts. Even if the accounts are in order, the accounting might not be. Attorney trust accounts should be transparent and they should be reconciled monthly. They should contain sub-accounts for each client who has money in trust, and you must be able to generate separate statements for each client.

In many states, banks are required to enter into a special reporting relationship with the state bar; banks may be required to report to the bar each and every overdraft or bounced check originating in an attorney trust account. Be obsessive about keeping good books. If you can't keep neat-looking books, at least keep honest ones. You can lose your license over any mishandling.

IV.

Practice Defensively
The Ten Commandments

1. Develop Relationships with Lawyers You Can Call on Regularly

A novice lawyer cannot have a successful solo practice without the assistance of experienced attorneys. You need a mentor, or a committee of mentors, who will listen to you and talk to you. You want lawyers who will show you how to do something or explain to you why you shouldn't. You might not need to consult on every case, but you will always need to bounce ideas off of someone with more legal experience.

Develop a relationship with someone who can see a larger part of the "seamless web," as Justice Holmes called the law. There will be times when you need to see something coming from around the corner. There will be times when there is a much easier way than yours to accomplish a result. There will be times when you learn something that *"every lawyer knows,"* and you wonder why you didn't know it. You need to have an experienced lawyer look over your shoulder.

While you must have confidence in your own judgment and ability, do not underestimate the vastness of the law, the complexity of practice, or the fallibility of your own judgment. If you do not know attorneys that you can call on, cultivate them.

Meet them wherever people meet lawyers and explain that you are going solo, and that you need an experienced attorney as a sounding board or second opinion. Most lawyers will be flattered. They will also recognize that the time commitment is minimal, and the potential benefit to them could be great.

"While you must have confidence...,
do not underestimate the vastness of the law,
the complexity of practice,
or the fallibility of your own judgment."

Often, retired or semi-retired attorneys would be glad to be your mentor. Ask around. It may be appropriate to make such an attorney "of counsel" to your firm. To some, it is an honor. It is not pretentious for a young attorney to associate with an older one, even if the relationship is principally honorary. In addition to having a friend in the business looking over your shoulder, having "of counsel" on your letterhead shows the world that you are not *really* alone. It can give you the appearance of being a *firm*, not just one sole lawyer. Make sure that anyone you would invite to be of counsel is an attorney that wants to help you. Your choice of counsel should be an always-available source of legal information and professional advice.

Before you determine what role, if any, counsel will have in your practice, check with the state bar rules and with your malpractice carrier and your worker's compensation carriers to see what will be required of you and of your counsel.

Your mentor should have a strong interest in your practice and an emotional stake in your success. Few people are born with those qualities. Cultivate them.   When you find attorneys who seem like good prospects, take the time to develop an interest in their practices. The best way to get lawyers to take an interest in your practice is to take an interest in theirs. Ask them questions about what they do. Get them to share tricks of the trade or war stories. Don't try to impress them with your few. Go out for coffee, lunch, a beer. See if the relationship is worth cultivating. Is this one of the people to whom you ask, *"May I call you sometime when questions or issues pop up that I'd like to discuss?"*

Even if you have found the perfect person to serve as counsel, you should always have a few other lawyers you can turn to. If you want to work in a specialized field, seek other lawyers in that field.   Try to see them as your colleagues, not your competition. In time, you may end up assisting these lawyers on their cases, or even getting referrals from them. Some day, when you have to refer a case to a colleague because of its complexity or a conflict of interest, you can pay back your mentor's kindness with a referral.

2. Know Your Stuff and Know Your Depth

As a lawyer, you will be approached by many people seeking your opinion about a host of varied matters. You will be sprinkled with questions concerning immigration law, enforcement of judgments, real estate, divorce, tax law, copyright and the Thirteenth Amendment.   No one can be an expert in all these fields. It's really okay for a lawyer to say, *"I don't know."*

Young lawyers are particularly reluctant to admit their uncertainty or ignorance of the law, especially to "civilians." This is dangerous. Happy is the lawyer who has learned to say, *"I don't know, but if you'd like, I could find out"* or *"I don't know, but I could put you in contact with an attorney who does."* You must decide whether you want to take the matter and become and expert on it, or refer it to someone who is already an expert.

If you decide to handle the matter yourself, immediately learn how to do it. That way, if you decide you are in over your head or that you can't stand that sort of work, you will have time to withdraw from the case without prejudicing your client. Be very careful about the cases that you decide to keep. Sometimes we take cases that interest or excite us, and we can't wait to sink our teeth into them and learn all we can about them. Other times we take cases that we don't care to handle, but we *really* need the retainer. This is dangerous.

Make sure that you are paid enough to allow you the time you will need to gain expertise. Do not charge under "market price" just because you have little or no experience with a matter. These are reasons to charge *more*. After all, you will probably spend far more time ascertaining the law and procedure on such a matter than a lawyer who has handled many similar cases in the past. Don't sell yourself short, but don't underestimate the amount of time you will need to get up to speed.

When you get a new matter, learn what you can about the laws and the procedures that are involved. You should know how to handle each case from stem to stern. If secretaries, clerks or paralegals work on your cases for you, know and understand everything they do and how they do it. Learn how court papers must be formatted. Then learn how they must get filed. Know who is entitled to receive copies and how the copies must be sent. You should be able to review your entire product for errors, omissions and compliance with rules. You should be able to take over the file at any given point. Achieving that competence is usually a matter of asking the right questions.

Sometimes a judge or a lawyer, or even a potential client will speak to you in mystifying terms or with anagrams you've never heard before. It may sound like, *"Counsel, have your client fill out the P-55 and take it over to Dora at FTG. If she does it today, we can do the UBH next week."* If you do not understand a local usage or a new anagram, stop the speaker (or wait until s/he's finished) and say, *"Excuse me, I am not familiar with that abbreviation,"* or *"I'm sorry, your Honor, I don't believe I know who Dora is."*   Don't try to fake it.   Of course, the best approach is to learn all you can about your matter beforehand from people who would know more than you.   Clerks, court officers and other attorneys will be glad to help you out, if you know what to ask and how to ask for it nicely. Civility is the key.

3. Say NO to Cases that Two or More Lawyers Have Handled Before You

Attorneys are often contacted by potential new clients whose cases have been reviewed or handled by another lawyer. Sometimes, the previous attorney will have withdrawn from the case.   Sometimes the client was dissatisfied with the attorneys' representation.   Sometimes, the client just can't afford the lawyer. Whatever the reason, whenever you are not the first attorney on the case, there is usually a red flag.   The case is not undesirable, *per se,* merely because another lawyer does not see its merit or does not want to represent the client. But beware.

> **"Whatever the reason, whenever you are not the first attorney on the case, there is usually a red flag."**

Any time an attorney turns a client away, or a client complains of problems with a former (or present) counsel, you should ask questions of client and counsel before jumping on board.   Far more often than not, the problem is with the client, and the current (or former) lawyer will often be quite frank if you call up and ask the questions directly.

Example: *"Hi, Ms. Lawyer. My name is John Henry, and a client (former client) of yours, Gina Jones, has consulted me about representing her in the case. She told me that you no longer wish to represent her. (Or, "She told me that she seeks to find new counsel to replace you.") The file appeared to be order, so I would like to talk to you about the case and the client. If you will need compensation for your services to date, please let me know your terms."*

By addressing the other attorney's fees early in the conversation, you assure him that you have his interest in mind. You may also learn critical information about the client.

It is a good idea, upon meeting such a client, to prepare an authorization (or limited waiver of confidentiality) for the client's signature that authorizes the existing or former counsel to discuss the client's case with you. It can be simple: *"Dear Attorney, This will authorize and direct you to discuss my matter freely with attorney Marc Garfinkle and to provide copies of my documents to him at his request. Thank you."* Have the client sign the original before she leaves your office.

As a courtesy to counsel, you may prefer to telephone the other attorney in advance, to advise that the authorization will be following. Most attorneys will be gracious. In fact, most attorneys will be relieved, hoping that you will, indeed, take over this problematic case or troublesome client.

Remember the general rule: If the client has already had unsuccessful experiences with two prior lawyers, you should avoid handling the matter at all. Lawyer Number Three rarely handles any matter to the client's satisfaction. Of course, if you are paid a substantial enough retainer to justify working with a problem client on a problem case, or you possess specialized knowledge or ability that neither of the other lawyers had, you may overlook the rule.

4. Recognize and Avoid Conflicts of Interest

Conflicts of interest are like poisonous snakes. We know we are to avoid them at all costs, but we know only vaguely what they look like. The kinds of conflicts that you are most likely to encounter are rather limited. They are nonetheless dangerous. The most obvious conflict is when we have a position adverse to that of an existing client. That is always to be avoided.

The most common species of conflict is when we have a position in a matter that is adverse to the interest of a *former* client.   Your new client is rear-ended by John Jones.   You represented Jones in a real estate purchase ten years ago. Can you still take the case? The answer used to be a clear "no." A lawyer was prohibited from taking a position contrary to the position of a former client. Even if the former client forgot ever having retained the attorney, lawyers would never take a case against a former client.

> **"Conflicts of interest are like poisonous snakes.**
> **We know we are to avoid them at all costs,**
> **but we know only vaguely what they look like."**

That has changed.   The U.S. Constitution now means that lawyers may no longer be held to higher standard of behavior than anyone else. In the past, we were required to avoid certain relationships, refuse to take certain cases, and otherwise act in a fashion that might look improper to someone who might draw the *wrong* conclusion.   The appearance of impropriety alone was tantamount to a conflict of interest. Accordingly, the states have dropped the requirement that attorneys must avoid the *appearance* of impropriety.   They must only avoid actual impropriety. It is still a good practice to avoid even the appearance that you are acting improperly.

The Model Rules of Professional Conduct, which may differ slightly from the rules in your state, are clear about what constitutes a conflict of interest with your client.

Rule 1.7 Conflict Of Interest: Current Clients
(a) Except as provided in paragraph (b), a lawyer shall not represent a client if the representation involves a concurrent conflict of interest. A concurrent conflict of interest exists if:
(1) the representation of one client will be directly adverse to another client; or
(2) there is a significant risk that the representation of one or more clients will be materially limited by the lawyer's responsibilities to another client, a former client or a third person or by a personal interest of the lawyer.
(b) Notwithstanding the existence of a concurrent conflict of interest under paragraph (a), a lawyer may represent a client if:
(1) the lawyer reasonably believes that the lawyer will be able to provide competent and diligent representation to each affected client;
(2) the representation is not prohibited by law;
(3) the representation does not involve the assertion of a claim by one client against another client represented by the lawyer in the same litigation or other proceeding before a tribunal; and   (4) each affected client gives informed consent, confirmed in writing.

There are several commercially available conflict-avoidance programs for attorneys. These help you to avoid taking cases against present of former clients. These are necessary in large firms or firms with numerous departments or old firms with many files. A solo can usually get along for years by checking for conflicts against an alphabetical file of clients, including the client's business names, if the client is a business owner. Your state bar probably has suggestions for conflict avoidance.

Whenever you have a matter against an individual or a business, you should check your potential defendants against your list of present and former clients. Remember, where a conflict exists, the client may waive it and allow you to proceed. As an attorney, you do not have that right.

If you learn enough about a potential new case to make you think that perhaps you have a connection with another involved person, do not proceed with the interview until you determine that there is no conflict, or get waivers as necessary, before you can proceed. You will, at some point in your career, be "conflicted out" of a handsome fee. When it happens, try to be philosophical.

Many young lawyers are surprised when they learn that going into business with a client is an ethical minefield. The possibility of abuse and of undue influence has led to many proscriptions against having an interest in a client's business. Read Model RPC 1.8 or your state's equivalent, to see the restrictions and conditions that apply.

> **"You will, at some point…, be 'conflicted out' of a fee.**
> **When it happens, try to be philosophical."**

There are other sorts of conflicts that you are likely to encounter if you work for the public. Soon after you hang out your shingle, you will be approached by two or three people who wish to form a partnership. Probably, only one of them will know you or knows someone who knows you. They will want you to draw up partnership papers between them. They have an idea of what they want, and they want you to make it legal. Legally, you are licensed to draft such an agreement. Ethically and practically, there are issues that militate against it.

Before you get far into discussing their plans, you should insist that each party be represented by separate attorneys. Rarely will partners have identical interest in an enterprise or have identical reactions to various terms of the partnership agreement. Accordingly, it is rarely acceptable for one attorney to represent two parties in the formation of a partnership or joint venture. Clients naturally assume that their partnership will succeed. Attorneys must remind them that it might not, and should prepare an agreement that protects their clients in either eventuality.

The overwhelming majority of partnerships do not succeed. Anticipate that the next time you see the partners together, the meeting will not be a happy one. You may also anticipate that the terms of the formation of the agreement will be called into question. Your will be cast as the lawyer for the partner that brought the matter to you. You could be called as a witness. You should refuse that job.

Sometimes, you may see a small matter, such as a request that you prepare an I.O.U in the amount of $300. The parties want a brief document to commemorate the debt and terms of repayment. Clearly, the size of the matter might not justify engaging one lawyer, let alone two, yet the ground rules have not changed. Be circumspect and defensive in handling these seemingly small matters. Maybe your mentor can help you out, here. That's another reason you need some.

Criminal cases are fertile territory for conflicts of interest. Sometimes two or more people have been arrested together for a crime or offense. They may be friends or family of each other, and they both come to you for representation. In almost every case where there are two or defendants, you will be able to imagine a situation where one person might be offered a benefit in exchange for help against the co-defendant.

It does not matter that the situation will *probably* not arise or that, if it did, the party would refuse the offer. What matters is that the situation *might* arise. Most judges will refuse to let you represent both parties. At the very least, it may appear to court and other counsel that you were fighting to keep both fees. That perception, alone, is one more reason to avoid this sort of conflict entirely. Withdraw with grace.

That said, there are times, particularly in municipal court, when the judge will hear your assurances that no actual conflict exists, and will allow you to represent more than one defending party. Unless there is a compelling reason to the contrary, it is rarely a good idea for one attorney to go to court with two defendants, even if the court allows it.

These conflict situations can be good for you. They may provide you with an opportunity to refer one of the conflicted parties to other counsel. You may get to pay back a favor that way, or start a stream of referrals with your "conflict counsel." When life gives you lemons, make lemonade.

Sometimes, conflicts arise *during* the handling of a case. You might learn something that compromises your client's position or your role as advocate. Your discovery may reveal that one of the witnesses against your client is a cousin of yours, or that the amusement park you are suing is owned by a company in which you have an interest. Keep alert to conflicts, and if you must withdraw your representation, do it at the earliest possible time. Do not try to hang on to the case or figure out a way to make money from it. Just get out.

5. Put it in Writing

It may not be long before you and your client, or you and your suite-mate, or you and your landlord have different understandings about the responsibilities of each. In spite of the written agreements you may have, there is still plenty of room for ambiguity, misunderstanding and confusion. The solution is simple. Confirm all of your significant agreements and understandings in writing. The more frequently you write things down and the more detailed you are, the less likely you will be to suffer the ill effects of miscommunication. Attorneys know countless stories in which note, an email, or a fax would have prevented confusion and/or ill will, or a malpractice claim.

> ## "Confirm all of your significant agreements and understandings in writing."

Look at an example involving a client. Most solos have had this happen. Suppose your client called you yesterday at 4:30 p.m. and told you about a new municipal court case she "picked up." She wants to know whether she needs a lawyer, and if so, what your fee would be. You told her to fax you the paperwork, you said that you would review what she sends, and you quoted her your "likely fee". You think she understood what you said, and she thinks you understood what she said. At 6:30 p.m., she faxes or e-mails you her paperwork, including the court notice. Somehow, the next morning, as you are in your office reviewing other papers, she calls to tell you that she is in court, waiting for you, and that she has half your money. All you remember is asking her to do is fax you the paperwork.

Even if you are representing someone on a simple matter for a small fee in a limited circumstance, it is still important that you prepare a written retainer agreement. Do so with each client on each matter. You may have great leeway in the contents of certain agreements, and the state bar may have very specific requirements for others.

Retainer agreements protect *you*, so use them.   Most states require that an attorney's fee agreement be memorialized in some sort of writing or it cannot be enforced by the attorney. Often sample copies of retainer agreements are appended to the court rules or the ethics rules. Some courts specify the language that must be used in certain specific retainer agreements, such as personal injury cases or divorce cases.   Whether you tailor each retainer to the client and case, or you keep a supply of different printed retainer agreements by your side, you should always put in writing your entire agreement with the client.

Perhaps because solos are frequently undercapitalized, they are sometimes understaffed and fail to do the little things that would have protected them. They don't write or dictate the letter telling the client that his case was dismissed or that the other attorney is requesting discovery that must be answered. Many claims against lawyers would be avoided if the lawyers just wrote more "confirming" letters to cover their backs. Make it a habit.

6. Review All Your Files Regularly

Many of the ethical or legal problems that confront attorneys would have been avoided if the attorneys had paid closer attention to the files. A few simple habits can help you stay on top of things. As a lawyer, you will not be heard to say that you were unaware of a deadline, or an exception, or the next step.   You cannot say that you didn't know the law or that you didn't read the letter carefully, though it was addressed to you.

> **"Many of the ethical and legal problems that confront attorneys would have been avoided if the attorneys had paid closer attention to the files."**

When you first get started, you may have only a few files, or a few handfuls, or a few dozen. You may not feel the pressure to review your files regularly, since you have such a finite caseload, and they are all on your desk right now.

You can protect yourself easily by reviewing all of your files regularly, preferably more than once a month, hopefully with a more experienced lawyer. That way, you will see problems before they get out of hand. Fortunately, there are not many situations where a clerical mistake or missed deadline, quickly discovered, will result in serious prejudice. The cases that burn solos usually have plenty of warning signs in the file. Rarely does such a problem arise where an experienced lawyer has recently reviewed the file.

In many firms, the associate or partner enters a "review" date on each file each time they put the file away.   On the appointed date, the secretary brings each such file to the lawyer's office for review.   Your system may vary from that. You may note your tickler 30 days out to review each file that you put away.

Another way to protect yourself is to devote a few hours to reviewing all your files at the same assigned time, weekly, biweekly or monthly - Monday early; Friday late; Saturday early. By establishing a routine in which you regularly review each file, you will not only avoid malpractice claims and perhaps even ethical ones, but you gain an opportunity to review the file for additional legal work that might be needed, and it may prompt you to send billing statements with greater regularity.

7. Avoid Having the Only Known Copy of a Document

Lawyers get in trouble when they are careless with their handling of documents.   Nevertheless, papers do get lost, destroyed and misfiled. For that reason we have filing systems and protocols that generally keep our files in order and our documents available. We should usually be able to retrieve documents in our files with relative ease. Even so, whenever you can, when you return the original of any document to the owner, keep a copy for yourself. Clients will remember leaving the original with you.

Clients will often bring important originals and copies of documents to you. If you have a general practice, you may get to review wills and deed, birth certificates, marriage certificates and death certificates. You may be handed a social security card, insurance policy, driver's license, gun permit or any of a host of other documents. If you must keep the original, give your client a copy with a receipt for the original. Make this your routine. It will protect you later.

If a client's document later is missing after a trip to the lawyer's office, the lawyer will be blamed. Fortunately courts, adversaries and clients are usually amenable to helping attorneys replace missing paper or recreate a file, but it is not without headache and heartache. Whether or not a document's disappearance was your fault, you don't want to have had the last known copy.

If you need to retain original documents such as trial exhibits, keep them in a separate folder in your file. Give copies to your client. Get a signed receipt for the copies, and note on your file jacket or computer file that you have original documents that must be returned. When you close the file, return the originals to the client. More than a few lawyers have closed their files, putting them in storage with important documents inside. Eventually, they have a time-consuming headache on their hands, and there is no one they can bill for it.

For similar reasons, do not let anyone leave or "drop off" documents for you, unless you know that the other person is retaining copies or the originals. Upon receipt of the documents, send a letter or email, acknowledging receipt, including language such as, *"Since I was not in the office to make copies for you, you advised me that you were sending me copies of the paperwork, and that you were retaining the originals. For reasons we discussed, I am not going to handle this matter. I will not be returning the copies."* Use receipts whenever you exchange documents with a client. Practice defensively. And, of course, put it in writing.

8. Communicate With Your Clients

By far, the most common source of dissatisfaction with lawyers is a lack communication, and particularly the lawyer's failure to return phone calls. Practicing defensively, you can see how easy that is to avoid. It has been estimated that two-thirds of the people who changed lawyers cited the lawyer's failure to return phone calls as one reason for changing. That should give you an idea of how to keep your clients. When you fail to call someone back, you are not only rude; you are suggesting that her matter does not have importance. At the same time, you suggest that nothing has been done on the file since the last call.

The irony is that many of the non-calling lawyers were probably handling their cases capably. They were doing a good job. Unfortunately, the client had no way of knowing that. Some busy lawyers figure that they won't report back until they have some news to report. This is bad. Call all your clients back the day they call, even if you have nothing of interest to tell them. You may have spent all week in court, or were out of town. Perhaps you were just waiting to review a report before getting back to your client or felt that there was no progress to report. Your client is not expected to understand this.

If clients deserve a call back, so do adversaries, judges and court clerks. Call them back the day they call, whenever possible. If you are unavailable, and you have a secretary, receptionist or other people who can make calls for you, have them return the calls or emails toward the end of the day, explaining that you are still unavailable but that you will call back as soon as you can. Then do it. People will be impressed by your accessibility.

Lack of communication also manifests itself as a client's failure to remember important parts of a conversation. Of course, their erroneous perception always cuts in their favor, for some reason.

For example, if you told a client that you MIGHT file a certain motion, the client will swear that you *promised* to do it. If you, in fact, DID promise to file the motion, the client will remember you promising *to win*. And if you were so foolish as to guarantee victory on the motion, the client will be sure that you were not going to charge a fee for the motion! It's often like that. Make sure that your client understands what is happening on his case *and* on his account. If your client understands what to expect concerning the case *and* your fee, he will be easier to please.

9. Control Your Clients' Expectations

Unhappy clients are the result of unfulfilled expectations. The problem of high expectations is nowhere more evident than with personal injury cases. Some such cases can be quite attractive, as they may not be too complicated for the novice attorney who has expert counsel and sufficient resources to handle the case professionally. In fact, most solos are amenable to handling good "P.I. cases," and many look to specialize in it. Few young solos would turn down or even refer out a serious injury case involving excellent liability and coverage.

Be careful of what you tell the client when you try to sign her case. Some lawyers find it easy to tell that severely-injured client that she has a "million dollar case." It even may look that way at first. Just bear in mind that there is no easy money. If a case looks like easy money, look at it again, with a more experienced attorney.

The first lawyer who tells the victim she can get her a million dollars will probably get the case. You know that could be you. And so you tell her. And you get the case. And already you are thinking about how to spend the fee. You may not know it, but three other lawyers she had spoken to told her that there was a problem with her case. A prior injury, an uninsured defendant, your client's history as a sex felon, a governmental immunity, an inconsistent statement – something was a problem with the case.

"Unhappy clients are the result of unfulfilled expectations."

The other attorneys were right. Now, it's time to settle or go to a costly, lengthy trial. You are offered $25,000.00. All things considered - liability, triability and collectability – you should jump at the offer. You realize that's the thing to do. Cut your losses. *Get something.* But your client says no. She even took all of next week off from work to help you prepare for trial. She still expects a million dollars. Have fun!

In injury cases, avoid discussing with your client the value of the case for as long as you can, following the injury. The value of the case depends on the extent of the permanent damage and disability. Before you assess the value of an injury, wait until all treatment has been rendered, and the injury has stabilized. You will need to review the medical records and reports, and research recent jury verdicts. Explain that it is too early for you, as an ethical lawyer, to predict the ultimate value of the case with any precision.

Of course, at some point toward the end of the case, the client has the right to know what you think his case is worth. And you should, by then, have a pretty good idea. After all, you are the expert, and the client will almost always defer to your opinion of an offer. You may be the expert, but estimate conservatively.

If your client's expectations are realistic but conservative, you will often have a happy client at the end. If your client is expecting pie-in-the sky, you will have a problem. Let him know early and often that his expectations are unrealistic. A client with unrealistic expectations may force you to try a case that should not be tried or move to be relieved because of irreconcilable differences with the client.

Similar principles apply in criminal court or traffic court. Make sure your client understands exactly what the "worst-case scenario" is. Granted, very few cases result in the worst-case scenario, but your client should be aware of what might be in store. Too often, judges ask a blanching defendant in traffic court, *"Didn't your attorney tell you that you could go to jail for this?"* Irrespective of whether they will actually be sentenced to jail, proper education of the client requires that you go over the worst-case, best-case and "most likely" scenarios with your client. Even if you are sure that your client will not go to jail, you must still inform him of the charges and their full implications. Then you should state what you expect the outcome to be.

Educating your client is the best way to maintain control of the situation. But some clients have their own agenda: they do not wish to be confused by the facts. How do you get an off-the-wall client under control? It may not always be possible to unbend a bent client, but *avoiding* the problem to begin with can be easy.

Try to spot quirky or eccentric clients and to keep a communication channel open with all of your clients. Keep your finger on your client's pulse. What does she want? What does she actually expect? How realistic is she? Note your file if you see untoward or undesirable reactions. Let her know your opinion. Keep her finger on *your* pulse, too. When an issue arises, discuss it with your client. Then put your position in writing. You and your clients will thus have fewer misunderstandings, and your client will appreciate your professionalism and concern.

Avoiding misunderstandings is particularly important in criminal, matrimonial, and immigration settings. These clients are often hampered by language issues or clouded by emotional issues. They have a way of not remembering warnings, sound advice or written agreements. You'll see.

10. Read the Ethics Rules and Keep Them Handy

Some states call them the Canons of Legal Ethics; others call them the Rules of Professional Conduct. Every law school teaches a course, and every state bar requires a test, to ensure that candidates for the bar know the ethical rules of the road. Despite that, thousands of lawyers each year flout the law and are charged with violating their ethical mandate. Many more didn't even realize there were ethics issues involved.

It used to be that a lawyer's negligence was simply a tort, remediable by the victim's claim of malpractice. A claim did not usually affect the attorney's ethics status or fitness to practice law. Attorneys accused of negligence had little fear of an ethics grievance for nonfeasance or malfeasance, especially if there was applicable insurance coverage. On large matters, they referred the claim to their Errors and Omissions carrier for handling. On small matters, they might have made an effort to settle directly with the client, before forwarding the matter to the carrier for handling. In the end, the client would be made whole, and the matter closed.

A perilous trend is emerging. Many of the actionable claims of attorney negligence involve errors and omissions that are also violations of the attorneys' code of ethics. Gross negligence, a pattern of negligence, lack of diligence, inadequate communication with the client, adversary or court, and other behavior suggesting attorney incompetence may also be ethical violations. Many common offenses, including dishonesty, lack of candor, impeding the administration of justice and similar misconduct may result in ethical charges by an adversary, a judge, or in most states, the Ethics Committee, itself.

The most common complaints involve a small handful of violations of this sort. Consider four of the *Model Rules of Professional Conduct:*

Rule 1.1 Competence
A lawyer shall provide competent representation to a client. Competent representation requires the legal knowledge, skill, thoroughness and preparation reasonably necessary for the representation.

Rule 1.3 Diligence
A lawyer shall act with reasonable diligence and promptness in representing a client.

Rule 1.4 Communication
(a) A lawyer shall:

(1) promptly inform the client of any decision or circumstance with respect to which the client's informed consent, as defined in Rule 1.0(e), is required by these Rules;

(2) reasonably consult with the client about the means by which the client's objectives are to be accomplished;

(3) keep the client reasonably informed about the status of the matter;

(4) promptly comply with reasonable requests for information; and

(5) consult with the client about any relevant limitation on the lawyer's conduct when the lawyer knows that the client expects assistance not permitted by the Rules of Professional Conduct or other law.

(b) A lawyer shall explain a matter to the extent reasonably necessary to permit the client to make informed decisions regarding the representation.

Rule 8.4 Misconduct

It is professional misconduct for a lawyer to:

(a) violate or attempt to violate the Rules of Professional Conduct, knowingly assist or induce another to do so, or do so through the acts of another;

(b) commit a criminal act that reflects adversely on the lawyer's honesty, trustworthiness or fitness as a lawyer in other respects;

(c) engage in conduct involving dishonesty, fraud, deceit or misrepresentation;

(d) engage in conduct that is prejudicial to the administration of justice;...

Fly straight, practice defensively, and you will sleep well as your practice grows.

They Don't Teach You THIS in Law School!

An attorney's ***pro bono publico*** efforts are an important part of any meaningful legal career.
It is our noblest tradition.
Offer your time and services to needy causes and individuals. This will remind you how important we are and how hard it is for people to access the system.

V.

Become a Lawyer's Lawyer

Marketing Yourself to Lawyers

Working for lawyers and representing lay people are vastly different. You may build a solid practice with either or both types of clientele. They are two distinct practices. The people you work for are different. They have different expectations of you, and you will serve them differently. Both can help you build your practice. A common progression is to start out working principally for lawyers, and to evolve into a practice that primarily serves the public. Of course, some attorneys who start out working *per diem* for other lawyers become associates or partners to one of the attorneys they served.

Approaching other attorneys for business should be easier than approaching civilians. You have a common bond and things you can always talk about (*"Where did you go to law school?"*) You can be less subtle about asking for business.   You may be direct when discussing terms. Lawyers should be able to get to the nitty-gritty without much tree-circling.

When talking to other lawyers about doing work for them, you must have a different mindset than if you are applying for a job. You are *not* applying for a job. You are equals. She is a lawyer. You, too, are an attorney who is also a business owner who provides services to lawyers such as she.

Promote yourself as you wish. Call yourself a *per diem* lawyer, a hired gun. You can sell yourself as a specialist or a jack-of-all-trades, a go-to-court person or a researcher, an appellate brief-writer or a discovery fiend. It doesn't really matter. You will succeed when you show that you can provide valuable services to that lawyer.

Traditionally, the most popular way to gain entry has been to work on a daily, or *per diem*, basis. We use the term *"per diem* attorney" to mean more than just attorneys who are paid on a daily basis. Attorneys who are paid by the hour, by the job or on a percentage are also called *per diems.* There is no standard arrangement. There is no standard job description, either.

Attorneys rely on *per diem* lawyers for all sorts of services. Some do insurance defense and use solos to cover depositions and motions for their insurance companies. With cutbacks in legal staff at the carriers, there may be more of this work available. Other lawyers know that they can charge their client much more than they will have to pay a *per diem* lawyer to go to court.

Some small practices rely heavily on part-timers, finding that a bevy of *per diems* is more cost-effective than building a equivalent-sized firm, with benefits and payroll taxes and the rest. If you can show a lawyer how to make more money by using your services, you can get some of that work. Be a research assistant. Be second chair at a trial. Attend discovery sessions. Cover courts and hearings.

There are many attorneys who do not use *per diem* help, but who would benefit if they did. When you meet them, suggest that they give it a try. Ask if they will allow you to work on just one matter so that you can show how you will make life easier for them. And bill them gently. You may get a client and another mentor in one shot.

In selling yourself, remember that you do not sell a product or service – you sell the result. Television ads don't talk about the dishwasher soap; they show you the streakless glasses and the smiling people at a dinner table. You should do the same thing. Figure out why the lawyer might use you, and tell her how good she'll feel knowing that the memo will be on her laptop when court breaks for lunch, or that she didn't have to cancel that deposition a third time on a case that should be pushed along.

Determine each lawyer's need. This is easy. All you have to do is ask. Don't talk about *your* practice; talk about *his*. Ask what he does, who is his clientele, what are his biggest problems. If he talks about being too busy or wanting more time off, or the endless waiting in court, or problematic deadlines, then you have ample reason to mention that your practice consists of helping attorneys with exactly the kind of problems he mentioned.

You are an intelligent, competent, ambitious, personable attorney who has the time and ability to help out other lawyers in different situations.   Many of the legal chores that are least enjoyable or least profitable to your prospects are new and exciting to you. You can spend time with their dreadful clients, so that they don't have to. You can organize files for use at trial, you can summarize depositions, appear in tenancy court or municipal court or even higher courts. You take small matters to trial. You can help them be two places at once.

It may be awkward when your very first prospect asks you for whom you have worked before. Don't waffle. Don't lie. Say something witty. Besides, it can only happen once.

Breaking the Ice

How do you find these lawyers and get to meet them? Assuming they are not already your close relatives, the best way is to have a friend or relative of that lawyer introduce you personally, complete with a handshake. If that's not happening, ask for a phone call or letter of introduction from such friend or relative to the lawyer that might pave the way for you.

No matter how you try to arrange introductions, do not let yourself be portrayed as a starving young lawyer who will do anything, even though that's exactly what you are. See to it that you are described as a sharp, versatile lawyer who does certain work for other lawyers. Take the card and recall the name of every person to whom you are introduced like this. Start a file of attorneys that you might call on later. Touch these cards again. Call or send a note to these people. Get remembered.

Personal contact is undeniably the surest way to be remembered. It is also the best way to get business. An important decision here is whether you wish to set up appointments with the lawyers whom you wish to solicit, or to "cold call" in areas such as office buildings or neighborhoods where lawyers are likely to abound. Call on the phone, or just drop by. Each approach has advantages and drawbacks.

The well-prepared cold call is the most efficient way to get business from lawyers. Just be ready to handle rejection. Prepare a letter introducing you, and bring many originals along with you. Don't forget to bring your résumé or c.v. If you are looking to work principally for lawyers in a specialized field, prepare a résumé that shows your focus.   Prepare general and specific résumés, if appropriate to your search. If you wrote some paper in law school that you are particularly proud of, bring it along. Also bring a writing sample that is *not* from law school.   Correspondence or research is perfect. If you have not one such writing sample from the real world, make one up. Prepare a fictitious demand letter, being clear that it is fictitious.

> **"The... cold call is the most efficient way to get business from lawyers. Just be ready to handle rejection."**

Your letter of introduction should be brief, easy to read and informative. Keep it professional. Avoid the "display ad" look. Write it on letterhead. You should make many copies, and put each one into an envelope. The letter might read: *"Dear Attorney: My practice consists of helping busy attorneys handle their caseloads or be in two places at once. I also appear in court, go to hearings, research legal issues and prepare court papers such as motions. I help attorneys get the problem files off their desks, and into the drawer with the closed files."* Take it from there. If you have a particular interest or preferred field of practice, mention it briefly.

Go to each lawyer's office and say, *"My name is Jim Johnson. I am attorney who helps other lawyers with their overload or problem cases. I'd like to have to opportunity to meet Ms. Kingsley for less than three minutes. If that would be possible, I'd appreciate it. If you'd like me to come back, I'd be glad to. In either case, please give her this letter of introduction and my card."*

Your appearance at the other attorney's office will, from time to time, prove serendipitous for her.   You'll hear, *"You couldn't have come at a better time!!"* and you'll walk out with some business that day.

Whether you set up an appointment, or are ignored, or are turned down nicely, have a business card or simple announcement ready to fax or email to the office. Similarly, if the attorney cannot or will not speak with you or is otherwise unavailable, send the card or announcement, anyhow, together with a very brief note.

Making appointments to meet attorneys is time-consuming and frustrating. You can do it by phone, by email, or by regular mail. By phone, you will have to get through each attorney's defense network, usually a receptionist and/or a secretary that screens the lawyer's calls. Keep your message short. Say something like. "*Mr. Jones. I'll be brief. I am recently admitted, and my practice consists of helping other lawyers move those ugly files they hate to work on. I also do per diem work and research and writing. I pride myself in being a money-maker for my attorney-clients. Please let me send you my card with my name and such, and please think of me when the need arises. If you'd like to meet me in person, let me know. I'd be glad to buy lunch.*" (If you *do* buy lunch, go someplace cheap; Jones will probably insist on buying).

If he's still listening, or has expressed an interest, you may point out, "*You do a lot regulatory work. I'd like the opportunity to assist you on a regulatory matter, at some point, if possible.*"

You may make many calls before you make an appointment. That's normal. When you do have an interested party, ask either the attorney or administrative person to please make the appointment as soon as possible. Don't worry about appearing not busy or too hungry. Saying, "*If it's convenient for you, I'm free now. I can be right over,*" has hurt very few young lawyers. That demonstration of ambition, flexibility, or both, may be just what that lawyer's office is looking for.

When you discuss your services, be prepared to discuss your fees without hesitating. Your fees should be well below the fee you would charge a personal client for similar work or a similar amount of time.   Your region and local economy will dictate the appropriate price range for you.   If you are unsure how much to charge, call some of the *per diem* attorneys who advertise in the law journals, and ask them what they charge.

You must prepare your own "fee" speech.   It might go something like this: *"I usually charge $100 per hour for research, and $400 per half/day in court.   My fee can be less for short appearances.   I charge the same for travel time, and I will bill you for costs, including $.30 per mile when I use my car."*

Contacting lawyers by mail, and particularly email, can be cost-effective and efficient (and you can prepare and send it even at night).   Avoid the appearance of a mass-mailing type of announcement. They are cheap-looking and undignified.   Target certain attorneys, grouped by specialty, location, proximity to each other, and write them, to discover their interest in meeting with you. To the extent you can, personalize each letter.   Mention the attorney's name, and spell it correctly.

Keep it short, but explain how you can help them add value to their practice.   Be clear about your availability and your rates. You may say, *"I will call you on Tuesday May 14, at 3:30 p.m. to learn whether you are interested in meeting."*   If you set yourself a deadline for calling, you should, of course, be timely.

Three advantages of making appointments are:
1. that the lawyer has already expressed an interest or need in your services;
2. you can learn about the particular practice and tailor your "pitch" for that firm; and
3. you can schedule several in a morning or afternoon, and allow time for travel between them.

One disadvantage is that attorneys are notorious for cancelling or changing appointments at the last minute. Roll with the punches.

No law says you must call yourself a *per diem* lawyer. You may have an entirely different approach to your prospects. Perhaps you want lawyers to refer you their conflicts or their overflow work. Perhaps there are matters that might seem like low-grade ore to a more established practitioner, but which handily meet your minimal criteria for new business. You can be of value to many lawyers in many ways. Let these lawyers know of your availability and your interest in working with them, and in meeting their colleagues who might also benefit from your services.

Business is hiding everywhere. Every lawyer needs some help with some matter at some time. Find those lawyers and give them good value. Your diary will fill up quickly.

They Don't Teach You THIS in Law School!

People who contact you by mail can usually wait several days for a response.

People who contact you by phone can often wait until the next day, as long as the matter is not urgent, and they're told you'll call back.

People who contact you by fax can usually wait a few hours, or even a day, for a response.

But people who contact you by internet expect a response within minutes. If you do not respond promptly to an inquiry, you will not get the case. If you use your website or email to get new business, have a host respond on your behalf or keep a constant vigil on your incoming email.

VI.

Developing a "Real" Clientele

Working for lawyers is fine, you say, but you want to have your own clientele. You want a "real" practice. But how do you build a clientele? Ten lawyers will tell you ten different "best ways" to do it. All will agree that prompt, high-quality service and a continuing effort to get business are essential.

It's *What* You Know

Understand that people want information much more than they want lawyers. So don't sell yourself as a lawyer. You are a resource, an expert, a source of information. You are someone they can come to for legal information. You may not have all the answers, but you know where to look and whom to ask when there are answers you do not have. People are, somewhat justifiably, afraid of calling lawyers for advice. They are afraid that they have "stupid questions" or that they may be charged for a consultation they do not need or for almost-good advice.

If they think of you as a resource, people will remember you when they need a lawyer. Being thought of as a friendly, reliable source of information is the surest way to get calls. Encourage the people you know to call you if they have questions you might answer with your legal expertise. Avoid begging or sounding desperate, and don't be heavy-handed, but tell people what you do and how you might help. Never try to talk someone out of their existing lawyer or compare yourself to him/her.

Hand Out Business Cards

Although many successful law practices have been built on business cards, it's hard to assess just how helpful business cards will be in building *your* practice. Don't take a chance. It's a numbers game, and it requires you to give away many cards in order to get results. Most get filed or tossed and are never seen again. From time to time, however, you will get a call from a new client or a lawyer who had your card or who knows someone who had your card. But cards serve a much bigger purpose than that.

Giving out your card extends and reinforces the ritual of meeting someone new. It adds a sense of permanency to the meeting. Sometimes, when you give your card, the receiver sees something in a name or an address that makes a connection which you never would have discovered with a mere handshake. You'll never know what business you *didn't* get because someone you met two weeks ago couldn't remember your name.

> **"Giving out your business card extends and reinforces the ritual of meeting someone new. It adds a sense of permanency to the meeting."**

Choose a card that is informative and conventional. High-quality, crisply-printed cards are best. It should be embarrassing for a lawyer to have a cheap-looking business card. It is a nice touch when the design of your business card is echoed in your letterhead. If your card indicates your credentials, specialties or other non-vital data, make sure that they comport with state bar requirements.

It is sometimes embarrassing, and occasionally costly, to be without your card. Never let that happen. You can avoid that situation by printing a sufficient number of cards and keeping some in your home, in your car, in your office and on your person. Keep them in each purse or wallet you use, and keep several cards in each of the jackets you wear.

Business cards are for distributing. Sometimes, you will want to give your card to someone, but you don't know how to do it gracefully. One way is to ask the other person for his or hers. When they give you theirs, offer yours. If they do not have one, say, *"Here, take mine and send me yours when you get back."* Of course, today you might download the information directly into your I-phone or Blackberry. But still do the card thing when you can. It leaves a more lasting impression.

When you hand out your card, only offer one or two. There is no reason to offer more than that unless you are asked. People rarely need more than two of your cards, and, if you give them a dozen, they will probably throw away all but one or two. Handing two cards is not offensive. Three is a bit much.

From time to time, you will meet people who will actively seek to send you business. Perhaps they have a business in town and will display your cards on their counter. When such people ask you for a stack of cards, don't be cheap. Give them a stack. But when you are handing your card to the average person or client or lawyer, one will do.

Don't Be Afraid to Ask for Business

Whenever you give out your card, use the opportunity to promote your practice. Don't just hand the card. Say something that refers to your practice. It can be as simple as, *"My office is right in the neighborhood,"* or *"I prefer the title 'lawyer' to 'attorney',"* or *"I handle accident cases – I hope you never need* me." Get the other person to look at your card. That might provide the extra second he'll need to remember you later on.

You will be in contact all day long with people – lawyers and non-lawyers alike - who may be inclined to refer clients or business to you. They are not likely to do so unless they know that you are looking for business. Let them know specifically the kind of work you are looking for, and that you can help people with certain types of problems. In time, you will find a variety of ways to come around comfortably to the topic.

Examples: *"You know, Ms. Jones, it was great running into you – my sixth-grade teacher – here at the mall. I enjoyed reminiscing. Before I go, I'd like you to take my card. Please remember that I am always ready to help someone who needs an attorney to help with his or her business. As a business attorney, I am often able to help out companies and business people in a variety of ways. I'd be pleased if you thought of me when someone mentions such a need. Please don't lose my card."*

"Thanks for the haircut. I'll be back. Nice job. (Hand a decent tip, of course). You're very professional. Your job is a lot like mine – you have to pay attention to detail and treat your clients well. I am a lawyer that specializes in zoning and land use. If you or someone you know ever has a question about a variance, I can probably help. Thanks again. May I give you another card, in case you know someone who might need my help? Let me write "zoning lawyer" on that so you don't forget."

Of course, you should entirely avoid asking for business when you know that the other person is presently represented by counsel in a matter. Remember the Golden Rule.

Send "Thank You" Notes

Keep a box of thank you notes by your desk. Use them for any appropriate occasion. Even create occasions to use them! The most obvious opportunity is to thank someone who refers a client to you or introduces you to someone who may be helpful to you. Send a thank you note assuring your sources that you will work hard to justify their confidence. Phone calls to say, *"Thanks"* are okay – they show your appreciation, but e-mails are even better, as the written word leaves a longer-lasting impression than the spoken one (and can be retrieved if the recipient ever needs to contact you again).

> **'Keep a box of thank you notes by your desk.**
> **Use them for any appropriate occasion.**
> **Even create occasions to use them!"**

Best of all is the written thank you note, especially if you take the time to write something personal. A thank you note will give you the opportunity to say, *"Perhaps someday I will be able to return your kindness – please keep me in mind."* Or, "I am enclosing my business card in the hope that I might someday be able to reciprocate," or *"As I am a bankruptcy lawyer, I hope you will never need my services; however, please think of me in the event that you know of someone whom I might help. I enclose my card."*

For many reasons, it is a good idea to keep track of the people (attorneys and others) who send you business. Sending a thank you note to the "source" of each new referral will help you to keep track of the people who think of you, even when the client ultimately does not retain you. Even where the potential client only calls or emails you, and you do not ultimately get the case, an appropriate note to the referrer is always in order. You might write something like this: *"Ms. Jones consulted with me as a result of your thoughtful referral. Although it does not appear that she will retain me in this matter, I appreciate your thinking of me and I will continue to treat the people you refer with courtesy and professionalism."* That is not overdoing it.

Thank you notes are particularly effective as marketing tools when the recipient has no reason to expect any thanks beyond that which you have already offered. If a lawyer at the courthouse explains a local practice or offers you a pointer or tells you what to expect from a certain judge, take that lawyer's business card and send a thank you note.

When a store clerk goes out of his way to locate an item, or a gas station attendant fixes the hanging license plate you didn't notice, send a thank you note and include your card, and send a note to the employer with a copy for the employee who gave you such good service. Even at a giant multinational corporation, the note will be put in the employee's personnel file, seen by her superiors, and the employee will never forget that nice lawyer who took the time to send the thoughtful letter.

Become a Resource for the Media

This is the Information Age. Media outlets are everywhere. There are TV, radio and print journalists that are crawling over each other for stories and analysis every time a news story breaks. Most stories have at least one, and usually several, legal angles. The media always interviews lawyers about everything.

You are certainly an expert in some fields of law, despite your inexperience. You might not get asked to appear on Court TV or CNN at first, but local journalists and local radio and cable show hosts might consider you expert enough to satisfy their audiences. You'll never know unless you submit your credentials.

Let's say you still remember a ton about Weights and Measures law, because of your Moot Course case. Prepare a letter to the various local media advising of your expertise and asking them to keep your name on file. Keep it brief. *"Dear Ms. TV Host or Reporter: Everyone I know counts on your show for timely interviews whenever there is a major news story. I am a local lawyer who can be a resource for you if you should have a story which touches on Weights and Measures law. I am enclosing my CV along with my card, which I hope you will file and remember in the future. My personal cell number is xxx-xxxx."*

Contact all the media people you can think of. Tomorrow's front page may be about shortchanging at the gas pump. You may also contact speakers' bureaus and bar association speaker panels, and sign on to give free talks on various legal subjects. You will expand your reputation, increase you experience at speaking to audiences, and you will gain credibility among your peers when you lecture to groups. State, county and local Bar Associations often maintain good public relations by offering, at no cost, an attorney to discuss matters of interest to that group. Not only is this fun, but it can lead to good contacts at the various places you speak, and it enables you to provide a bit of *pro bono* service back to your bar association and to your community.

Have you seen how thin newspapers have become? They are begging for content. Help them out. With less trouble than you might think, you can write a regular column for the local paper or community bulletin. Prepare a series of short (500 words or so) articles on legal matters of interest to your community. Prepare at least five or six. A dozen would be best. Submit them to your local paper with an offer to prepare them regularly if the paper will give you a regular column. You should be entitled to a "by line" with your office information and specialty.

> **"With less trouble than you might think, you can write a regular column for the local paper."**

Networking Groups

Although they have been around for many years, business networking groups such as BNI and LeTip are finally being recognized as mainstream business marketing tools. Essentially, these groups consist of business owners and professionals who meet regularly, such as every week or every other week, to advance their businesses. A group might include a printer, a restaurant, an accountant, a travel agent, a general building contractor, a roofer, a real estate broker, a real estate lawyer, a matrimonial lawyer, an insurance agent, a stock broker, etc.

Membership is restricted to one person from each profession or specialty, and they agree to use each other's services or products. More importantly, the members learn about each other's businesses so that they can promote them within their respective circles of friends and family. In essence, each member of the group becomes a sales person for each other, insinuating their co-members into their own spheres of influence. A good networking group is like "word-of-mouth" on steroids.

Lawyers are taking full advantage of this marketing-by-networking scheme. Even large firms are sending people from particular specialized legal departments into the networking groups. Typical legal specialties that are represented in these groups are real estate, immigration, estates and probate, personal injury, employment, and family practice. However, there are still parts of the country, and parts of each state, where a general practitioner can make a good living through success at networking.

Whether you have a general practice or a specialty, you should look for a group that has several other lawyers. Generally speaking, the lawyers in the group are far more likely than the "civilians" to refer business to you.

Organized networking is one situation where your lack of experience may work against you. You may not have a long enough list of satisfied clients to qualify for membership. Also, it may be difficult for members to "sell" you if you have very limited experience. If your professional resume is short, rest assured that it won't long stay that way. In the meantime, you might want rack up some battle scars and look at networking groups again in a year or so. You are probably not far from a BNI chapter. They have almost 6,000 chapters. Check them out online (http://www.BNI.com) and go to a meeting.

A Word on Internet Networking

In addition to the networking done at lunches and business meetings, millions of people are "meeting" on the internet. The ability to disseminate information to friends and friends of friends in nanoseconds has changed marketing entirely. Websites allow us to connect with our own networks and those of others with a few clicks of the mouse. This has not been undiscovered by lawyers. There is no stronger trend in the legal profession than the move to internet marketing.

They Don't Teach You THIS in Law School!

Whenever your adversary requests an adjournment,
an extension of time, or any other courtesy,
you should agree unless your client will be harmed.
You may need a favor tomorrow, and you don't need a
reputation as a jerk. Don't let your client call this shot.

There is a big difference between meeting potential clients on the street and having them find you on the internet. Clients who find you on the "net" may not know about your honest smile, your warm, firm handshake or your stentorian voice. People who meet you everywhere else will know all that. But clients who find you on the internet will know where you went to school, what organizations you belong to and what your practice emphasizes. People you meet on the street will not know that. Therefore, when you are preparing you website, emphasize your credentials and have a good photograph. That is how you will be judged. The handshake comes later, when you meet them on the street.

LinkedIn, Avvo, Plaxo and others are social networking groups, based on the internet, that cater to business owners and professionals. They can be valuable tools for promoting your business, but they have limitations for attorneys. For example, a LinkedIn member may be willing to open her list of contacts to you, but, as a lawyer, you can not directly solicit them. Other professionals are not so restricted. Nevertheless, these groups have many ways to help you publicize your practice and to direct business to you. It is worth your effort to explore them.

Even before you open your office, you should consider using networks such *Facebook for Business* and *LinkedIn* to publicize your professional plans and to look for helpful connections. You have the time to let people know what you are hoping to do or trying to find. As more people learn that you are opening an office or looking for a special situation, more good things can happen. People know people who know people. The more "chatter" there is, the more connections you will make.

About Joining Organizations

Traditionally, lawyers joined civic, charitable and religious organizations in order to develop contacts. There are school-based, church-based and town-based groups. Almost all of them need help doing work in the trenches. There is a constant shortage of volunteers. Lawyers are often called upon to serve as Trustees or Committee people in these organizations and are often given leadership opportunities quickly. If you can volunteer your time, you may move to prominence in the group, enhancing your prospect of making favorable business contacts and building your clientele.

Some groups attract many lawyers, all hoping to do the same as you. Only a few will succeed at growing their business through that organization. It is a common mistake to join several groups in the hope of enlarging your network. The attorneys who succeed at getting significant business from a group, club, or organization, will almost always be the lawyers who are active within the group. Your co-members might not think of you if you are a member in name only, and you just show up for the banquets. It is far better to devote your time to one or two causes where you become known for your dedication and hard work.

They don't teach you THIS in law school!

When you send an important letter or email, most people who open it will not read past the caption.

So, whenever you write to a clerk or court or insurance company, put your caption in **boldface** with enough information to tell the whole story.

Properly done, the body of your letter can be short.

Here is an example of a good caption to the court:

Re: Jones vs. Harding   Dkt: XXX-L-2010-53892
Plaintiff's First Request to Adjourn Conference
(for discovery reasons)
Present Date of Conference: March 17, 2011
Proposed New Date: June 1, 2011
Judge: Hoolihan
Adversary's Consent: yes

Dear Clerk:

Politics Can Help

Many lawyers get involved in politics. We are naturals. Who is better prepared to deal with legislation and argumentation? The notion that you will make important business contacts through politics has a lot of support. Of course, so much depends upon you. Local political parties are usually looking for volunteers and contributions. Contributions are easy to come by. Volunteers are not. Volunteering will cost you less and yield better results than just giving a check, unless, of course, you can write a very LARGE check. Typical opportunities for you will be stuffing envelopes, getting people out to vote on Election Day, and working on fundraisers. Writing letters and attending political meetings will also get you noticed.

Sometimes, working on the local or county level might gain you recognition that will result in an opportunity to serve in an appointed office or to run for elected office. Political involvement has brought success to many lawyers. At the least, it should create some additional name recognition, a phenomenon that causes people to like you or dislike you, even passionately, although they've never met you. Ah, politics.

There are side benefits to a political life, as well. Involvement in politics, whether on the local, county, state or national levels, will keep you abreast of events and make you interesting. It might put you in touch with people who can help your career. It will give you a greater stake in your community.

Sometimes, political involvement might help you land you a job such as municipal prosecutor or public defender, or even a judgeship. In any event, politically active people strengthen the fabric of democracy. If you can gain business or a paid position by working with a party, think of it as your bonus for supporting the American political system.

But be careful. Politics can be a trap for the wary and unwary alike, and no one will hear lawyers say that we were unwary. Be careful of the attachments that come along with success in politics.

Work on Your Business Every Day

There is an adage that it is better to spend time *on* your business than time *at* your business. Understand what that means. We often get so involved in performing the tasks of our various caseloads that we neglect ensuring the survival and growth of our practices. We see ourselves as attorneys first and business people second, so our practices take back seat to our caseloads.

At the end of a long day of computer and paperwork, meetings and appearances, phone calls and emails, we delight when our work day is finally over. This is a dangerous attitude. The solo cannot afford to ignore her business, even for a day. Make business-building your constant concern. You need not be obsessive about this, or even spend much time on it, but success will not elude you if you do something, however minor, to help your business seven days a week.

> **"We see ourselves as attorneys first and business people second, so the practice takes back seat to the caseload."**

"Working on the business" can be as simple as tweaking your website, writing a blog that may bring you attention, or reading about the business of being a lawyer. It can mean creating a newsletter, publishing an article or column, attending a networking group (more on this elsewhere), speaking to civic or special interest groups, or assisting at a charity event. It can be as much fun as touching base with old friends on *Face Book*, updating your *LinkedIn* profile, adding an endorsement to your website, or meeting a client or prospective client for lunch.

Computers provide great and varied opportunities to work on your business at night, on the weekends or when you are suddenly inspired. Newsletters, websites, and blogs can be prepared in advance and published as desired. Organize these files intelligently, and you will be able to re-use, recycle or revise the pieces in the future with less effort. Develop the habit of working on your business daily, and you will reap the rewards forever.

Marketing to an "Ethnic" Clientele

Most Americans have at least one national, regional, racial, religious or tribal identity besides "American." These cultural identities are characterized by skin color, religious traditions, ancestral garb, nationality, diet, language, or some other identifier.

You retain a natural empathy for those who share your roots. You may eat traditional food and give to your children names which echo their heritage.

Frequently, we live in neighborhoods among people who share our ancestral customs and speak the language of the "old country," who attend the same houses of worship, and who shop at markets that sell hard-to-find foods and cultural accessories. Every significant city in America has more than one such community within it. For want of a batter term, "ethnic" defines these specific communities that you may wish to serve.

Ethnic communities are easy to reach with your message, since they are finite and often localized. You will get good bang for your promotional buck and more impact from your marketing time than with a broader market. You may even change your vision of your practice.

Ethnic and linguistic bonds are strong. If you speak the same foreign language as your clients, or have a common religion or fraternal lodge, your inexperience may never become an issue. Just knowing the right words to say when you walk into a room can give you instant credibility that even twenty years at the bar could not buy. Many lawyers have learned new languages just to better serve local clients. Some attorneys have even been known to change their name back to a more traditional spelling or pronunciation of an "ethnic" name that had been "Americanized" by prior generations.

> **"In a sense, you can specialize in that community, rather than in any substantive area of law."**

Even if you're not "ethnic," you may still earn the same advantages. Many communities of "recent" immigrants have not yet produced their own lawyers, and are underrepresented at the bar. Understand their needs. Learn about their cultures, their ethnic and personal histories, their problems and their expectations. Embrace the community. Support it. They will respect and honor you for choosing to work for them.

Like many solos before you, you may do exceedingly well by confining your reach to local ethnic communities. Advertise in the foreign language press or TV, and announce that your office is in their neighborhood or that your office speaks their language. Remember, however, that becoming popular in such a community almost condemns you to a stint as a generalist.

In a sense, you can specialize in that community, rather than in any substantive area of law. You will gain an understanding of the legal problems and issues that they confront. They will have questions of real estate and municipal court. They will retain you for traffic court and divorce court. You will prepare Powers of Attorney, "corporate kits," and leases both residential and commercial. They will carry your card in their wallets.

Depending on your clientele, you may learn a lot about taxi medallions, gas stations, liquor licenses, the restaurant business, health care workers, dollar stores, motels, or some other field of law that touches a large part of "your" community. In time, you may develop a niche or specialty from that knowledge, which specialty can extend your focus beyond your ethnic clientele. *Bonne chance, amigos.*

They Don't Teach You THIS in Law School!

If you should be called on to defend a client in a criminal case, particularly a trial, remember that many defendants come to court alone. This may suggest to others that your client has no one who cares about him. The judge or jury may deduce that no one likes him or that he is a bad person. Perhaps everyone that he knows is working and unable to attend, but you don't get to explain that.

So, when you have a trial in a criminal case, it may help if your client invites a few friends and relatives to go to court with him on the critical day(s). These people should be nicely dressed, and must remain perfectly quiet and well-behaved in court. They send the message that the client has people who care. It CAN make the difference.

VII.

Going to Court – A Primer *

(*Adapted from the author's *The New Lawyer's Hip-Pocket Guide to Appearing in Court* ©2009Marc Garfinkle, all rights reserved)

Lawyers wear many hats, play many roles, and serve many functions. Yet, of all that we do, our highest calling is representing a party in court. Courtrooms are still the domain of lawyers. *Courtrooms* are where our society's values are defined and our government's policies are tested. Courtrooms are where our bitterest disputes are resolved and our notion of justice is made manifest.

Some lawyers go a lifetime without setting foot in a court. Others go to several courts each day. Other lawyers may spend weeks, months, or years in a given courtroom. You may be seeking a career that brings you often into court. A general practice almost guarantees some court time for you. It will be fun, if you do it the right way.

Maybe you've just been given an assignment by a lawyer you just met, or you're actually been retained by a paying client. Unless you are asked the question directly, you should not volunteer that you've never been to court before, or that this is the first of this type of case that you've done. Why shake your client's confidence, when you know that you will do a top job? Maybe it's a name change or a final judgment of divorce. Perhaps you've been hired to fight a traffic ticket or clear up an outstanding warrant. The assignment is well within your ability as long as you know the ropes, even if you never did this sort of thing before.

You must appear in a certain court at a certain time. The client will meet you there. The client expects you to know what to do and how to do it. You've discussed it with two other lawyers, and with your adversary, and you know just what is supposed to happen. You can know your stuff, but can you look professional presenting it in court?

Law school does not prepare us for going to court. No one teaches this, but good lawyers eventually all learn it. There are many things about going to court that you have to learn on your own; maybe there are a few you can learn from a book. But first, you have to get to court.

Unless you have a reliable GPS in your car, immediately get directions to the court and include a copy in your file. If the court is a municipal court, ascertain that you have determined the correct municipality in order to avoid confusion with another municipality of same or similar name. Also, if the matter involves a summons issued by a police officer, the "date to appear" in court may not be a court day at all. It always pays to call the court to confirm.

You should also note all court appearances in your diary with a "tickler" the day before. Use this tickler to remind you to confirm your appearances for the following day (or Monday); don't count on courts to always notify you of schedule changes. Also, be sure to remind your client of the appearance. If a client fails to appear in court, some judges require proof that the attorney notified the client in writing of the date. It is a good practice to do so, even if not required. Email, if your client has it, is the best way to keep in touch about court dates and adjournments.

Allow plenty of time to get to court. Whenever possible, avoid travelling to the court with your client. If your appearance is less than successful, few clients will be fun company on the drive back. It is far better to meet the client at the court.   Carry the judge's or the court's phone number with you on the file jacket or in your cell phone. Give the number to your client, as well. If you are stuck in traffic or otherwise going to be late, all courts appreciate the call.

It is *usually* a good practice to be on time for court. As you gain familiarity, you may learn of particular courts or judges where attorneys need not appear until 10:00 as long as the client appears by 9:00, or where a phone call requesting a "ready hold" marking is acceptable. These are often criminal courts, where one prosecutor will be in court for the entire session, or workers' compensation courts, where an insurance attorney may spend the entire session with one judge. Judicious use of such information may save you countless hours over a long career, but don't plan on being late unless you are sure of the jurisdiction and the judge. Even in those courts where it's "okay" to be late, you should always call and leave word that you expect to be there at a certain time.

Lawyers usually dress professionally. Clients often don't. Make sure your client knows how to dress.   Attire should be professional. No hats, no sunglasses, no fancy jewelry, no sneakers or casual shoes.   Although courts and counsel vary, it is never a *bad* idea for men to wear jackets and ties, and women to wear dresses, skirts or pantsuits. Some courts still discourage pantsuits for women. If you have any doubts, call the court clerk or a lawyer who might know, beforehand.

Going through the metal detector is at the threshold of a courtroom experience. Many courts, particularly urban courts that handle criminal cases, now have two metal detectors.   One machine scans *objects* that are placed on a conveyor belt; a larger machine, adjacent, scans *people* as they pass through. Sometimes, a magnetic wand is used instead.   If you have an Attorney Identification card, keep it where you can find it quickly.

There is always at least one attorney who passes awkwardly through the metal detector, or who repeatedly sets off a metal detector and doesn't know why. He looks amateurish to the client. Let this not be you. Remove any belt with a heavy buckle. Place all your metal objects, cigarette packs, keys, metal pens, cell phones, Blackberries, and coins into the tray or dish provided for that purpose. If you have a coat or jacket or briefcase, you may place these items into a pocket or into the briefcase. The tray, coat or briefcase can then be passed through the machine which sees the contents.   You may then walk through the machine without looking like it's your first time.

It is a good habit to greet and chat with the court officer, the clerk, the prosecutor, and other court personnel, even when you are in a court that is new to you.   You may well be back. People remember you, usually favorably, if you take a moment to acknowledge them and talk to them. The dividends are subtle but rich. When you walk into a courtroom where you haven't been in months, and the officer at the metal detector greets you with a familiar, *"Good morning counsel. How have you been?"* you'll feel good, and your client will be impressed.

There is another important reason for you and your client to always be polite to the court staff: judges quickly hear of any perceived rudeness. You may have been entirely correct last week on the phone, and the court's staff may well have been inept, dishonest and evil. Their stupidity may have cost you or your client time and money, their rudeness may have been appalling; but keep a cool head and a civil tongue. More than a few judges have initiated an appearance by asking, *"Was that _you_ who spoke so rudely to my administrator, counsel?"* There is no good answer.

> **"Don't be embarrassed to question other lawyers...**
> **It is better to plead ignorance to a colleague than to**
> **demonstrate it in front of a client."**

Cellular phones present new assaults on courtroom decorum. Signs at the doors advise people to turn off their cell phones in court. An officer, or the judge herself, will warn the public of harsh penalties for violations. Still, there is always one person whose phone rings, usually with a ridiculous ringtone. You don't want to be that person. You don't want your client to be, either.

Leave your cell phone outside in the car or turned off and in a briefcase. Much like the attorney who holds up the line at the metal detector, the attorney (or client) whose cell phone sounds during court will be disdained by all for the balance of the day. You can do without those bad vibes in the court when your client's case is called.

If you are scheduled to appear in a court that you've never been to, or you are handling a matter that may be handled in a variety of ways, get the lay of the land in advance. Do not be embarrassed to question other lawyers or the court clerk or a court officer. It is better to plead ignorance to a colleague than to demonstrate it in front of a client. Learn all you can before you sit down in the courtroom. Lawyers are not like plastic surgeons who've patented a new procedure. We gladly share our trade secrets with colleagues. Take advantage of that.

Find someone who might know how the court, or this particular judge or prosecutor, handles the sort of matter you have. Ask whatever questions you have. You may learn valuable additional information, too. You may find out that you have at least an hour before the judge will hear you, that the arresting officer is on vacation, or that you don't need to put more quarters in the parking meter after noon on court days. You may learn what kind of mood the prosecutor is in, or that the judge is in a hurry to get to his daughter's soccer game. Knowledge is power.

No court appreciates "spectators" who converse while court is in session. Do not talk to the client or other lawyers in the courtroom. If you must speak, leave the courtroom and discuss the matter in the hall. While seated in court, avoid reading material, even your file, and do not send text messages from the court.

Avoid appearing casual. Keep arms off the bench backs and both feet on the floor. Some courts reserve some seats in front for attorneys. You may choose to sit there or to stay with your client. Play it by ear.

> **"Lawyers are not like plastic surgeons who've patented a new procedure. We gladly share our trade secrets with colleagues. Take advantage of that."**

If your client will be requiring an interpreter or a sign-language or hearing accommodation or if someone in your party has a medical condition the court should know about, advise a court officer or administrator at the earliest practical moment.

Often, the first impression a court will have is when your client's name is called at the roll call. Since we always stand when speaking to the court or when spoken to by the court, roll call is no exception. When your client's name is called, you should stand and say, "Present with counsel," or "Ready for respondent," however it is done there. The court may not yet need to know who you are. That comes shortly.

Eventually, it will be *your* turn. If yours is not the first case, you should pay attention to how other counsel approach counsel table. There are usually one or two approaches to the counsel area. Plan yours. It is bad form to cross a courtroom between the judge and the public. If you must leave the courtroom or move to a different part of it while another matter is being heard, avoid walking in front of the judge, even if it means going around the entire courtroom.

As you stand, make sure that you are not disheveled. Men should quickly make sure that their shoes are tied, and that their suit jackets are buttoned and fly zippers are closed. Women should straighten their dresses or skirts. Purses, backpacks or handbags should left at your seats when approaching. If this is impractical, look to the court officer to indicate where to place the bag.

If yours is the first case called, you may not know where you should stand. In a courtroom with a jury box, the state or plaintiff usually takes the position closest to the jury. If you are at counsel table with a client, the client generally stands to your side which is farthest from the center. In other words, if you are on the left of center, the client is to your left; on the right, your client is to your right.

Remain standing until the judge directs you to be seated. Stand with heels together and toes a bit apart, "at attention" but less rigid. Keep your hands at your sides, so you may use them freely if you gesture. Using your hands expressively is appropriate, and may be persuasive. Do not rock back and forth or hang on to the podium.

Under no circumstances should you or your client have your hands in your pockets. It is not only inappropriately casual, but it may raise a security issue. Correct the situation before the judge or court officer does.

It should be obvious (but apparently it isn't) that chewing gum should be eschewed by clients and attorneys in the courtroom. Not only does gum-chewing obscure your speech, it does little to enhance the impression of intelligence that you and your client are trying to convey. Park your gum outside.

If you have not submitted a written notice of representation with the court, or if you have only faxed one shortly before, it is a good idea to bring one with you to the court to offer at the time your case is called. Normally, the first thing a judge will say, once you are standing at counsel table or the podium is, *"Appearances, please counsel"* or *"State you appearances for the record, please."*   In criminal cases, the prosecutor states her appearance first; in civil cases, the plaintiff generally does.   In motion practice, the moving party or petitioner speaks before the answering party, defendant or respondent.

When announcing your name to the court, speak slowly and clearly. For some reason, lawyers race through their names as if they are embarrassed by them.   All too often, an attorney announces his/her name at counsel table, and the clerk, the court reporter and other lawyers in the courtroom glance around to see if someone caught counsel's name.

Take at least twice as much time to say your name as you normally would. Practice it a few times out loud. Even if it sounds funny to you, it will not sound funny in court.   Spell your last name for the record, particularly if your name is unusual or spelled in an atypical manner. The court or the court staff will appreciate your assistance.

After you've stated your name and your firm's name, indicate your client's name and relationship to the matter. Introducing a corporate client or business entity may require some verbiage at the front door. *"Good afternoon, Your Honor. I am Georgia Peach from the Law Offices of Bloom, Flowers and Dye, representing Joe's Hot Dogs, Inc.. At my right is Frank Furter, Vice President of Operations for Joe's Hot Dogs."*

Courts are occasionally duped by imposters, so your client may be asked to provide proof of identity. Remind your client to bring a form of photo identification.

Your client's (or witness's) testimony may require that s/he make an oath or affirmation. Explain to your client or witness in advance what that means. Some courts no longer offer the Bible for swearing. Others forget to offer the option to affirm, or to state under penalty of perjury, that the testimony will be true. You should find out in advance whether your witness will swear or affirm. When your non-swearing witness is instructed to raise her right hand and put her left hand on the Bible, you may interrupt with, *"She will affirm, thank you."* Not a problem. They will ask her, *"Do you affirm that the testimony…"*

"The judge's name is "Your Honor…"

You and your client should rise whenever the judge stands up or enters or leaves the courtroom. This is invariable unless the court or court officer directs that you remain seated. If, for any reason, you wish to remain seated during a proceeding where you would normally stand, ask the court for permission, directly: *"Your Honor, may I remain seated during my examination of the witness?"* Your request will rarely be denied.

The judge's name is "Your Honor," although you may refer to the judge as "the Court" or "the Bench." Never say "you" or "your" when addressing the court. You may see lawyers refer to the judge on the bench as "Judge." That is incorrect. "Judge" is familiar. "Your Honor" is the appropriate title. You may call a judge, "Judge" in chambers, in the hallway, at a child's birthday party or at the supermarket. On the bench, however, the judge is always, "Your Honor."

Clients or witnesses who may be questioned by the judge should be instructed to say, *"Yes, your Honor,"* and, *"No, your*

Honor," although it is not disrespectful for a lay person to refer to the Court as "Sir" or "Ma'am."

When before the court, *all* remarks are addressed to the court. Comments should never be directed toward opposing counsel or the client. We do not refer to our adversaries as "he" or "she." We give them names and labels. We say "counsel" or "the respondent" or "Mr. James." We rarely have reason to look in our adversary's direction.

Although we normally address the bench, the judge may direct us to do otherwise. For example, a judge might say, "*Please elicit a factual basis from your client, counsel,*" meaning that the court is directing you to *voir dire* your own client on the record to establish that there is a legal basis for his/her guilty plea.

If a party addresses a remark to you directly (e.g., "*Well, did you bring the transcript with you?*"), look directly at the court. You may ask, "*Shall I respond, Your Honor?*" If the court indicates that you are expected to respond, you should address the court, "*Your Honor, I have (or don't have) the transcript with me in court today.*"

If there is a cardinal rule, one even more sacrosanct than to stand when addressed by the court, it is that one should never interrupt the court. When a judge cuts us off, there is a tendency to want to finish what we were saying. That is a dangerous tendency. Judges seem more irked by this particular *faux pas* than by almost any other breach of courtroom decorum.

If there *is* a time when it *may* be acceptable for counsel to interrupt a speaking judge, it is when the judge has clearly misstated something or has made an incorrect assumption, and all counsel will agree that it was a misstatement or error. It is never easy to be the one who stops the judge, although the judge may prove to be appreciative. One way to do that is to stand up and

Clients are the lifeblood of your practice and the source of your future wealth. They will also be the cause of your insomnia, the trigger for your fury, the reason you had to miss the party and so much more. Your best and your worst experiences as a lawyer will almost certainly involve clients. Therefore, choose your clients carefully. Working for yourself, you will have that freedom. The problem is that it takes time before you learn to smell trouble as it walks through the door. Keep trying, though.

> **"Your best and your worst experiences as a lawyer will almost certainly involve clients. Therefore, choose your clients carefully."**

Look out for the early warning signs of trouble. Be suspicious of eccentric-seeming people and those who seem negative about most matters and people they discuss. Beware of clients who bad-mouth their former attorneys. Clients with obsessive-compulsive disorder will bring you many times more information or evidence than you will need, and will call you daily. They are usually intelligent and cooperative, but hard to please. You will have clients that may need assurances that you have not joined the "conspiracy" against them. You will have clients that believe that the mere hiring of a lawyer guarantees a rosy outcome. Others are just looking for someone to sue. Still others just want to tell their story to a captive audience. Learn to spot all of these types, and more, because they will find you. Yes, they will.

On the other hand, do not accept a bad or marginal case merely because you like the client. Continue to cultivate the client, but don't represent her. Treat her well, and she may remember you, but don't take that bad case just because you like her, or because you would like her future business. You won't win her loyalty based on your handling of a lousy case, no matter what she promises.

Lawyers have some traditions or habits that have been passed down through the generations. Not all are meritorious. For example, lawyers often refer to our clients as *"my guy"* or *"my gal."* We all do. "Guy" may be the neutral gender, because it seems to be okay to call a female client *"my guy,"* too. It is now accepted usage in almost every circumstance where lawyers discuss cases. You will do it, too, but refrain from using that expression around civilians; it sounds crass.

> **"Saying 'my client' reduces your client to a neutral commodity and costs you the opportunity to give your client a more sympathetic label."**

We have a similar habit in court. Lawyers constantly refer to their clients as *"my client."* Even top attorneys do it all the time. It feels great to say *"my client"* the first time you have your own client, but after that, the expression is demeaning. Every time you refer to the person or company that is paying you, you should use the opportunity to make them look good. Saying "my client" reduces your client to a neutral commodity and costs you the opportunity to give your client a more sympathetic label.

Especially in front of a jury, you want to humanize, not dehumanize, the person at your side. Call her, *"Ms. Jones."* Call her *"the unfortunate Plaintiff"* or even the *"Respondent"* or *"this poor, scared woman."* Allow her to have a connection to the case besides the fact that she is paying your fee.

That said, there may come a time when the mercenary nature of your relationship is exactly the connection you wish to reinforce. You may say, *"Your Honor, if the Court does not dismiss the case today, my client will have to come back again from Europe at great inconvenience and expense."* Now, she's your "client."

Don't Say a Word

Attorney-client communications are both confidential and privileged. The issue of confidentiality will arise frequently throughout your career. As a lawyer, you will hear other lawyers discussing their clients' matters indiscriminately. Names, characterizations, and seamy details. Attorneys do this all the time. It is still wrong. Some lawyers appear oblivious to what they are doing. Others do it coyly. The more illustrious or famous the client, the more likely it is the attorney will mention the name.

Even where there appears to be no harm in mentioning the facts, the prohibition stands. Watch what you say. The attorney is not the judge of which confidential communication or information may or may not be revealed.

The Model Rules of Professional Conduct set forth a general standard that many states have adopted *ver batim*.

Rule 1.6 Confidentiality of Information
(a) A lawyer shall not reveal information relating to the representation of a client unless the client gives informed consent, the disclosure is impliedly authorized in order to carry out the representation or the disclosure is permitted by paragraph (b).
(b) A lawyer may reveal information relating to the representation of a client to the extent the lawyer reasonably believes necessary:
(1) to prevent reasonably certain death or substantial bodily harm;
(2) to prevent the client from committing a crime or fraud that is reasonably certain to result in substantial injury to the financial interests or property of another and in furtherance of which the client has used or is using the lawyer's services;
(3) to prevent, mitigate or rectify substantial injury to the financial interests or property of another that is reasonably certain to result or has resulted from the client's

commission of a crime or fraud in furtherance of which the client has used the lawyer's services;

(4) to secure legal advice about the lawyer's compliance with these Rules;

(5) to establish a claim or defense on behalf of the lawyer in a controversy between the lawyer and the client, to establish a defense to a criminal charge or civil claim against the lawyer based upon conduct in which the client was involved, or to respond to allegations in any proceeding concerning the lawyer's representation of the client; or

(6) to comply with other law or a court order.

You will often hear it said that an attorney may reveal a matter learned in the course of the attorney-client relationship, if that matter is already, *"a matter of public record."* Don't count on it. Check out the RPC, above. Public record or not, you may still be revealing something your client did not wish you to mention, and not everyone is aware of the entire public record. In general, the habit of using clients' names is dangerous.

> **"Revealing a client's identity or**
> **discussing a client's legal matters with others**
> **are excellent ways to lose a client,**
> **lose the respect of your peers,**
> **and maybe lose a lawsuit."**

Lawyers, especially solos, love to swap "war stories." We talk about cases, clients, adversaries, friends, judges, juries, victories, and all else. Telling war stories is part of the fabric of being a litigator, a lawyer who goes to court. We get a chummy feeling as we regale each other with tales of our prowess or cleverness or courage in the face of horrendous odds. When you discuss a client's case with other lawyers, keep your client anonymous.

Revealing a client's identity or discussing a client's legal matters with others are excellent ways to lose a client, lose the respect of your peers, and maybe lose a lawsuit. As an attorney, you are entrusted with information. Often that information may be significant to others. Sometimes it may be harmful to your client. You will not know that your audience has a special interest in the information, or that it may be used against your client in ways you could not have imagined. The mere fact that your audience is a lawyer does not excuse your breach of confidentiality.

Similarly, maintain complete confidentiality around your spouse, your family, and your best friends. You are never free to discuss a client's affairs.   Not at the kitchen table, not at depositions, not in your sleep. If your wife's friend comes to see you with a minor problem, there is no need to mention it to your wife. The friend may do that. You may not. If you understand that there is no such thing as a *minor* breach of confidentiality, you will be better off. Loose lips sink ships.

They don't teach you THIS in law school!

Trying cases and arguing motions
present many learning opportunities.
Would you like to bring your personal "skills mentor"
with you to court to offer critiques and suggestions?

Not a problem. Almost every court has police or security
people in the courtroom. In trial courts, these people
get to see the best and the worst of the local lawyers.

Before you begin a trial or argument, or after it's over,
ask the officer for feedback. You can learn a lot from
helpful court officers, but they'll never volunteer. So ask.

Attorney-Client Privilege

This is really the *client* privilege.   Remember that. The attorney-client privilege means that you must refuse, even under oath, to disclose any conversations or correspondence or reveal any information that arose in the context of your attorney-client relationship.   The privilege belongs to the client. The client may waive the privilege; the attorney may not. Most states recognize exceptions where an attorney is suing the client for a fee or where the attorney is defending the client's malpractice action. The issue of "attorney-client privilege" usually arises in the context of litigation or criminal defense.

Representing Family and Friends

All solos, at some point, represent family members, friends or indigent people on a no-fee or low-fee basis. It often seems like the right thing to do. Yet most lawyers would agree that the best way to ensure having problems with a case is to do it for nothing or for very little.

If your intent is to do charity, fine. Chalk it up as *pro bono* work. But the cases you handle for friends or family or at a deep discount are the cases which, for reasons unknown, will defy resolution or will require ten times the normal effort. Ask any solo.

It may be difficult to turn down the starving widow or the favorite, but thrifty, uncle who trusts only *you*. It may be hard to charge your relative a fee, to refer a downtrodden clergyman to legal aid, or to tell your best friend that you lack the specific expertise he needs. You may even lose sleep worrying whether your "client" will get representation at all.

Get over it. It is not your problem. It is better to lose sleep over that than over a malpractice suit against you from a case you did for nothing. If this seems like harsh advice, do your good deed, if you must, but figure on having problems. In any event, it is a good idea to keep handy a list of Legal Aid offices and of other legal service options that may be available to people who call for, but cannot afford, your services.

IX.

Getting Paid

Fees and Retainers

That's what it's all about, right?   Of course, you expect to get paid for your work. Nevertheless, lawyers work countless hours each year for clients who will not pay them. Such clients will find you, too. They take many forms. Most of them are short of money. Some are short of morals. They may try to bargain your fee in the beginning or propose time payments that will survive your completion of the matter.

Be tough. When you quote a fee or figure out what is required, assume that every case is going to be a headache. When a potential client fusses about the amount of your retainer fee, explain that all you sell is your time and your expertise, and that proper handling of the case will require both. Get paid in advance whenever you can.

> **"In criminal cases, where payment plans are not uncommon, there is a general rule: Make sure that your *first* payment is sufficiently large that you won't kick yourself if you're never paid another dime."**

In some circumstances, such as personal injury matters, you may be able to accept a case on a contingent-fee basis, if you have the resources and sufficient expertise. This can be safely done when you know that there is insurance available to pay your client and your fee. Many states have the contingent retainer form mandated by statute or rule.

Some clients will want you to agree to a "payment plan." Here again, you must be the judge of your debtor. Is it worth the risk? In criminal cases, where payment plans are not uncommon, there is a general rule: Make sure that your *first* payment, the one you must receive before you will go on record as counsel, is sufficiently large that you will not kick yourself if you are never paid another dime.

An example is a fee of $2500 for which you will probably go to court once or twice, in addition to whatever other work will be required. You want the case. The client and her spouse are both employed. You're pretty sure they'll keep their word to pay. You are also pretty sure that they are prepared to go elsewhere, since they really don't have the money.

You might consider offering a payment plan consisting of a $1500 first payment plus $150 in trust for expenses. Ask for, say, a $500 payment in thirty days and another $500 thirty days later. Make sure the client believes the schedule is realistic. Then, of course, put it in writing. A payment plan is not ideal, and should be strenuously avoided, but if it passes muster under the "first payment" rule, take the case. If not, leave it.

If you are not paid as promised in a civil case, most judges will let you out of the case on a simple motion alleging non-payment. The client can represent herself unless or until she hires another lawyer. In a criminal case, where there is a Constitutional right to an attorney, getting out may not be so simple. A judge may not want to burden the state with providing your client her next lawyer. It may be harder to get out of the case. For this reason, the "first payment" rule developed.

Except for collections, never handle business or personal litigation on a contingent basis. Always insist on a retainer. Most retainers are considered an advance against hourly fees. In most states, they are paid into the attorney trust account, and the attorney then bills that account when the work has been completed or case-related expense is accrued.

> **"Except for collections, never handle business or personal litigation on a contingent basis. Always insist on a retainer."**

Many states have forbidden the one-time non-refundable retainer fee that merely guaranteed the lawyer's engagement, but bore no relationship to the work performed. For some matters, it may make sense to work for a specified reduced hourly rate, and a small contingent percentage; this is often called a "hybrid" fee.

The Model Rules of Professional Conduct answer the most common questions about fees:

Rule 1.5 Fees

(a) A lawyer shall not make an agreement for, charge, or collect an unreasonable fee or an unreasonable amount for expenses. The factors to be considered in determining the reasonableness of a fee include the following:

(1) the time and labor required, the novelty and difficulty of the questions involved, and the skill requisite to perform the legal service properly;

(2) the likelihood, if apparent to the client, that the acceptance of the particular employment will preclude other employment by the lawyer;

(3) the fee customarily charged in the locality for similar legal services;

(4) the amount involved and the results obtained;

(5) the time limitations imposed by the client or by the circumstances;

(6) the nature and length of the professional relationship with the client;

(7) the experience, reputation, and ability of the lawyer or lawyers performing the services; and

(8) whether the fee is fixed or contingent.

(b) The scope of the representation and the basis or rate of the fee and expenses for which the client will be responsible shall be communicated to the client, preferably in writing, before or within a reasonable time after commencing the representation, except when the lawyer will charge a regularly represented client on the same basis or rate. Any changes in the basis or rate of the fee or expenses shall also be communicated to the client.

(c) A fee may be contingent on the outcome of the matter for which the service is rendered, except in a matter in which a contingent fee is prohibited by paragraph (d) or other law. A contingent fee agreement shall be in a writing signed by the client and shall state the method by which the fee is to be determined, including the percentage or percentages that shall accrue to the lawyer in the event of settlement, trial or appeal; litigation and other expenses to be deducted from the recovery; and whether such expenses are to be deducted before or after the contingent fee is calculated. The agreement must clearly notify the client of any expenses for which the client will be liable whether or not the client is the prevailing party. Upon conclusion of a contingent fee matter, the lawyer shall provide the client with a written statement stating the outcome of the matter and, if there is a recovery, showing the remittance to the client and the method of its determination.

(d) A lawyer shall not enter into an arrangement for, charge, or collect:

(1) any fee in a domestic relations matter, the

payment or amount of which is contingent upon the securing of a divorce or upon the amount of alimony or support, or property settlement in lieu thereof; or

(2) a contingent fee for representing a defendant in a criminal case.

(e) A division of a fee between lawyers who are not in the same firm may be made only if:

(1) the division is in proportion to the services performed by each lawyer or each lawyer assumes joint responsibility for the representation;

(2) the client agrees to the arrangement, including the share each lawyer will receive, and the agreement is confirmed in writing; and

(3) the total fee is reasonable."

Whenever possible, have your client agree to pay all expenses in advance or as they come due. Check your ethics rules for the requirements for withdrawing from a case, and make sure your agreement includes the most liberal terms for your withdrawal. It is far better to get out of a case when you are owed a small sum, than to end up in litigation over a large one.

> **"Whenever possible, have your client agree in writing to pay all expenses in advance or as they come due."**

Interestingly, since the advent of caller ID, we have learned that when clients owe you money, they won't pick up the phone when you call; when they are fully paid up, they are eager to take your call. Make it easy on them. Don't take I.O.U.s.

You are competing for business against many other able lawyers. It is tempting to think that your ability to offer low prices may help you acquire some business. As a lawyer, however, your pricing should never be your best selling point.

Price your services fairly. Figure out how much you need per job, per appearance, per hour, per day – however your practice runs. Insist on a fair fee. Clients want a good lawyer more than they want an inexpensive one. Make sure that they understand how and when you will bill them, and how much it will probably cost. As with any important conversation you have with clients, confirm your understanding in writing. Remember, if there is any ambiguity in your arrangement, it will be resolved against you.

Many lawyers sign up with a bank or credit card company to take charge cards at terminals or on-line. People who would otherwise not have retainer money available may prefer to use an attorney who accepts credit. Sometimes people want to use the card just to get the free airline miles. The downside is, of course, the cost, with most credit card companies charging a fee per use as well as a monthly charge and other charges that you should monitor closely.

Shop carefully for credit card services. Equip yourself with a realistic estimate of the amount of credit transactions you anticipate, the average value of those transactions, and whether you will be promoting your services through a website. Generally, clients who find you on the internet are more likely to use a credit card than others.

Whether you take a retainer up front or send out statements for work you've done, develop a workable system for billing. There are many commercial legal billing programs available, but you may be comfortable devising you own. Ask other attorneys to discuss with you their billing systems; you may find one that works well for you.

Whether you bill by the job or by the hour, whether you are on a monthly retainer or billing against an advanced fee you have received, send out statements regularly. If your bills are submitted regularly, your lay clients and your lawyer clients will sense how serious you are about getting paid, and you are less likely to lose track of receivables before they become uncollectable.

Fee Disputes and Fee Arbitration

Lawyers traditionally avoid suing clients. It never looks good to the bench or the bar when an attorney fee dispute is brought to the court. If a client owes you a small amount of money for fees, walk away from the debt, and be thankful that the lesson was not more expensive. If the client owes you a lot of money, figure out what you did wrong.

> "It never looks good to the bench or the bar when an attorney fee dispute is brought to the court.
> If a client owes you a small amount of money,
> be thankful that the lesson was not more expensive.
> If the client owes you a lot of money,
> figure out what you did wrong."

Avoid getting into monthly or weekly payment plans, particularly with new clients. Clients who have paid you as requested in the past, or who have referred other clients to you, may merit your consideration for credit. But protect yourself. Get any payment plan in writing and leave yourself an exit route if you are not paid by a certain time or in a certain fashion. Check with your local ethics counsel or with other practitioners for language that will be enforceable in your state.

Unfortunately, fee disputes are a two-way street. Attorneys complain against clients who don't pay their bills, and clients complain that they have been overcharged or that the attorney's work was substandard. These cases are increasing in frequency.

In an effort to keep these matters out of court and, hopefully, to streamline them, most state bar associations offer some form of attorney's fee dispute resolution vehicle. Typically, attorneys and non-attorneys sit on a small panel and listen to both sides. They review the work that was done, they consider the result, and they make a binding or non-binding ruling as to the fee. In some states, an attorney who seeks payment *must* proceed through such a service, while the client may do so or may opt for the usual civil remedies for breach of contract. In either case, a compromise is usually the best way to have closure.

They don't teach you THIS in Law School!

The easiest way to collect a judgment is to
levy on the debtor's bank account
But judgment debtors try to hide that, soooo....
If you ever need to discover a checking account number,
think of a pretext to send the other party a check
in a very small amount.

*"Dear store: My client shoplifted a five dollar item and
feels guilty about it. Our check ($5.00) is enclosed."* or
*"Dear gas station, When I was in your waiting room today,
I broke your ash tray by accident.
Please accept my ten dollar check. Sorry."*

They WILL deposit your check.
When it comes back, you should find the
debtor's current bank account number
stamped neatly on the back!

X.

Worst-Case Scenario:
Parlay Your Solo Practice into a Real Job

Some young lawyers decide to go solo each year because no jobs that were available appealed to them. Others do it just to see whether they could make it on their own. Still others, undecided on a career path, and unsure whether they would enjoy lawyering, take on some part-time legal work just to check it out. They meet with varying degrees of success.

Successful or not, after a year or so in the marketplace, most of these lawyers will have a clear idea of what it means to practice law. They will also be far more qualified than before to seek employment with a law firm or with a corporation as house counsel. All will be able to offer employers a measure of legal and business experience they lacked when they first entered the market. In their year or two as solo, some even develop specialties or find some other professional niches that suit them. Many make contacts that will pay dividends for years.

To lawyers and clients alike, there is a world of difference between the new attorney, fresh out of law school, looking for her first job, and the solo, frustrated or otherwise, who is looking for a "straight" job. Failing to succeed at your own private practice does not signal failure at all. You may have learned how to run a law office; you may have mastered some of the ins and outs of going to court; you may have become adept at client development. Maybe you launched a popular blog.

You will probably have some clients who will return, even if you relocate or restructure your practice. Some of these clients will need you on an occasional basis; others, more regularly. In any profession, a job candidate who already has a clientele is generally more desirable than one who does not.

If you are back job-hunting after undergoing the trial by fire of solo practice, you may be surprised to see how much more impressive your resume has become. You now have recent legal experience in several fields.

You have thought about what you've done as a solo, and you can articulate the knowledge and skills and lawyerly traits you've developed or discovered. Good time-management habits. Reliable. Good judge of character. Persuasive advocate. Finds simple solutions. Relates well to...(...management, immigrant clients, politicians, young associates, the country-club crowd). Internet whiz. Rainmaker. Uses good judgment under pressure.

Arriving at a place where we talk about résumé-writing in a book such as this may seem like stepping back to Square One. It isn't. It is a measure of how far you have come and how much you have learned as a solo lawyer, even if you did not succeed at the business of lawyering.

Working as a lawyer without a job is not an easy path. However, the trip and the destination are both worth the effort, and the rewards you can reap from having tried the solo route are available nowhere else.

The legal landscape has undergone many changes in your lifetime. Law firms are bigger. Alternate dispute resolution is replacing litigation. Legal research is done by computer or by people under contract in India. Courtrooms are more casual. Attorneys are often less civil, and our collective professional reputation has never been worse. Specialties have come and gone. General practitioners, who were going, going, not quite gone, are now coming back.

The landscape will continue to change, and you will see changing opportunities and different visions of success. You will make connections and find work. With a tailwind, you may find success as a solo.

Wherever you practice, alone or with others, *pro bono* or big bucks, the core advice of this book holds true:

Practice defensively and intelligently. Choose your clients judiciously and charge them fairly. When choosing cases, stay within your comfort zone. Handle your caseload expeditiously and ethically. Seek advice frequently from other lawyers. Treat your colleagues with civility and camaraderie. Strive for a great reputation.

While you're at it, try to have fun. Take your freedom and do amazing things with it. Enjoy life after law school. That's what it's there for. Going solo is only the vehicle. Enjoy the ride.

MDG

Afterword

In 1976, a second-year law student at Hastings College of Law in San Francisco, already with a few part-time jobs, talked himself into yet another job – this time as law clerk to a lawyer whose father/partner had recently died. John F. Shirley, Jr. was overwhelmed with work, and I was honored to help him out. I had no idea that my life was about to change.

John immediately gave me his old office, his old Dictaphone, a 35-hour per week caseload, direct access to his legal secretary, and minimal guidance. To almost any substantive or procedural question, John would usually reply, *"Figure it out. You're the lawyer!"* I missed countless classes, but I couldn't have had a better teacher.

As a qualified student law clerk in California, I was allowed to appear in court, so I tried two small cases for John. Winning one, and settling the other after the entry of proofs, I was as effective as the "real" lawyers. I thought I could even do it alone. Then, I attended a seminar by Gerald M. Singer, Esq., who had recently written the seminal book, *How to Go Directly into Your Own Solo Practice without Missing a Meal.* That was it. My direction was set. I passed the bar. I hung out a shingle. I have rarely looked back, and I haven't missed a meal.

Marc Garfinkle

APPENDIX

**Table of Contents of the ABA's
Model Rules of Professional Conduct**

Advocate

Rule 3.1   Meritorious Claims and Contentions
Rule 3.2   Expediting Litigation
Rule 3.3   Candor toward the Tribunal
Rule 3.4   Fairness to Opposing Party and Counsel
Rule 3.5   Impartiality and Decorum of the Tribunal
Rule 3.6   Trial Publicity
Rule 3.7   Lawyer as Witness
Rule 3.8   Special Responsibilities of a Prosecutor
Rule 3.9   Advocate in Nonadjudicative Proceedings

Transactions with Persons Other Than Clients

Rule 4.1   Truthfulness in Statements to Others
Rule 4.2   Communication with Person Represented by Counsel
Rule 4.3   Dealing with Unrepresented Person
Rule 4.4   Respect for Rights of Third Persons

Law Firms and Associations

Rule 5.1   Responsibilities of a Partner or Supervisory Lawyer
Rule 5.2   Responsibilities of a Subordinate Lawyer
Rule 5.3   Responsibilities Regarding Nonlawyer Assistant
Rule 5.4   Professional Independence of a Lawyer
Rule 5.5   Unauthorized Practice of Law; Multijurisdictional
             Practice of Law
Rule 5.6   Restrictions on Rights to Practice
Rule 5.7   Responsibilities Regarding Law-related Services

Public Service

Rule 6.1   Voluntary Pro Bono Publico Service
Rule 6.2   Accepting Appointments
Rule 6.3   Membership in Legal Services Organization
Rule 6.4   Law Reform Activities Affecting Client Interests
Rule 6.5   Nonprofit and Court Annexed Limited Legal Services
             Programs

Information About Legal Services

Maintaining the Integrity of the Profession

Index

About the Author

Some thirty years ago, Marc Garfinkle had just been graduated from Hastings and had passed the California Bar exam. He wanted to practice in San Francisco. But he loved his independence, and he *really* didn't want to get a law-firm job.

Already working one part-time job as a private investigator and another one teaching and lecturing, Marc figured he only needed a few hours at lawyers' rates to bridge the weekly gap and make a survival income. A year earlier, he had been going door-to-door in San Francisco's neighborhoods selling fire alarms. Now, he would try to sell his legal services. He began by soliciting lawyers. Knocking on doors. Leaving letters. Making connections. Finding mentors. He found work: making appearances, prepping their clients, trying small cases. Then, somehow, while no one was looking, Marc's practice grew.

Today, Marc Garfinkle is a civil and criminal trial lawyer with over thirty years of experience. He is Adjunct Professor of Persuasion and Advocacy at Seton Hall University School of Law and is on the teaching faculty of the National Institute for Trial Advocacy (NITA). He is a member of Phi Beta Kappa (Marietta College), the National Association of Criminal Defense Lawyers, the American Association for Justice (formerly American Trial Lawyers' Association), the New Jersey State Bar Association, and the Association for Continuing Legal Education (ACLEA).

Marc is a past Chair of the New Jersey Supreme Court District VB Attorney Ethics Committee, and is the Public Defender in Livingston, NJ. In addition to *"$olo Contendere,"* Marc has written the popular *"Hip-Pocket Guide to Testifying in Court,"* and the *"New Lawyer's Hip-Pocket Guide to Appearing in Court."* He has written numerous law-related articles and is a frequent guest on radio and television.

"You sel dwet pa manje kalalou."

Haitian proverb:
"With just one finger, you can't eat (slimy) okra."

I could not have succeeded as a solo
without the help of attorneys on two coasts.
Muchas gracias to my friends and colleagues
John Shirley, the late Norman Ascherman,
the late Benjamin L. Bendit, Mark S. Tepper,
George Engler, Howell Lovell, Jr.
and Harvey L. Weiss.

Merci to my long-time friend, Bob Bly,
who knows everything about publishing.
Asante to legal technology guru Ari Kaplan
for selflessly sharing his knowledge and his contacts.
Grazie to coach Mark Riesenberg for helping me focus.
For pointing me toward the solo path,
Salamat po to Walt Whitman.

And thank you, thank you, thank you,
students, faculty, and administration at
Seton Hall University School of Law
for restoring my faith in the future of our profession.

No words in any language can thank my wife, Eylana,
for her patience and understanding
during the preparation of this book,
or our children, Yaël and Jordan,
for their unflagging confidence
that I had something of value to offer.

M.D.G.

Made in the USA
Columbia, SC
08 July 2019